BILLIE HOLIDAY
SINGER

ARTISTS OF THE HARLEM RENAISSANCE

REBECCA CAREY ROHAN

Cavendish Square
New York

Published in 2017 by Cavendish Square Publishing, LLC
243 5th Avenue, Suite 136, New York, NY 10016

Copyright © 2017 by Cavendish Square Publishing, LLC

First Edition

No part of this publication may be reproduced, stored in a retrieval system, or transmitted in any form or by any means—electronic, mechanical, photocopying, recording, or otherwise—without the prior permission of the copyright owner. Request for permission should be addressed to Permissions, Cavendish Square Publishing, 243 5th Avenue, Suite 136, New York, NY 10016. Tel (877) 980-4450; fax (877) 980-4454.

Website: cavendishsq.com

This publication represents the opinions and views of the author based on his or her personal experience, knowledge, and research. The information in this book serves as a general guide only. The author and publisher have used their best efforts in preparing this book and disclaim liability rising directly or indirectly from the use and application of this book.

CPSIA Compliance Information: Batch #CS16CSQ

All websites were available and accurate when this book was sent to press.

Library of Congress Cataloging-in-Publication Data

Names: Rohan, Rebecca Carey, 1967-
Title: Billie Holiday : singer / Rebecca Carey Rohan.
Description: New York : Cavendish Square Publishing, [2017] | Series: Artists of the Harlem Renaissance | Includes bibliographical references and index.
Identifiers: LCCN 2015036039 | ISBN 9781502610621 (library bound) | ISBN 9781502610638 (ebook)
Subjects: LCSH: Holiday, Billie, 1915-1959. | Singers–United States–Biography.
Classification: LCC ML420.H58 R64 2016 | DDC 782.42165092–dc23
LC record available at http://lccn.loc.gov/2015036039

Editorial Director: David McNamara
Editor: Amy Hayes/Elizabeth Schmermund
Copy Editor: Nathan Heidelberger
Art Director: Jeffrey Talbot
Designer: Stephanie Flecha
Production Assistant: Karol Szymczuk
Production Editor: Renni Johnson
Photo Research: J8 Media

The photographs in this book are used by permission and through the courtesy of: The Library of Congress @ Flickr Commons http://www.loc.gov/rr/print/195_copr.html#noknown)/ File:(Portrait of Billie Holiday, Downbeat, New York, N.Y., ca. Feb. 1947) (LOC) (5020399920).jpg/Wikimedia Commons, cover, 78; Bill Spilka/Getty Images, 5; Harry Hammond/V&A Images/Getty Images, 6; Public Domain/File:Billie Holiday 1917.jpg/Wikimedia Commons, 10; Courtesy Peter Sefton, 13; Gilles Petard/Redferns/Getty Images, 15; Hulton Archive/Getty Images (background, used throughout the book), 17; Michael Ochs Archives/Getty Images, 18, 37, 47, 61; JP Jazz Archive/Redferns, 21; Carl Van Vechten/The Van Vechten Collection, Library of Congress/File:Bessiesmith.jpg/Wikimedia Commons, 22; Peter Newark American Pictures/Bridgeman Images, 24; Popperfoto/Getty Images, 29; Bill Spilka/Hulton Archive/Getty Images, 34; Rex Hardy Jr./The LIFE Picture Collection/Getty Images, 38; DON EMMERT/AFP/Getty Images, 40; The Library of Congress @ Flickr Commons /http://www.loc.gov/rr/print/195_copr.html#noknown)/ File:(Portrait of Billie Holiday and Mister, Downbeat, New York, N.Y., ca. Feb. 1947) (LOC) (5020400274).jpg/ Wikimedia Commons, 44; Fred Morgan/NY Daily News via Getty Images, 49; John D. Kisch/Separate Cinema Archive/Getty Images, 52-53; Jack Delano/Library of Congress/ File:JimCrowInDurhamNC.jpg/Wikimedia Commons, 55; Photo © AGIP/Bridgeman Images, 56-57; Nat Farbman/The LIFE Picture Collection/Getty Images, 62; Edward B. Marks Music Company, 65; Julie Alissi/J8 Media, 68; Keystone-France/Gamma-Keystone via Getty Images, 71; Charles Peterson/Hulton Archive/Getty Images, 74-75; Metronome/Getty Images, 83; Alnum/Newscom, 86-87; Harry Hammond/V&A Images/Getty Images, 89; Keystone-France/Gamma-Keystone via Getty Images, 92; The Library of Congress @ Flickr Commons (http://www.loc.gov/rr/print/195_copr.html#noknown)/ File:(Portrait of Billie Holiday, Carnegie Hall, New York, N.Y., between 1946 and 1948) (LOC) (5020400014). jpg/Wikimedia Commons, 96; Bob Parent/Hulton Archive/Getty Images, 99; NY Daily News via Getty Images, 101/ Evan Agostini/Invision/AP, 107; Courtesy Christine Cochrum, 108; AP Photo/Rob Carr, 110-111; Sergey Goryachev/Shutterstock.com; Pictorial Press Ltd/Alamy Stock Photo, 113.

Printed in the United States of America

TABLE OF CONTENTS

Part I: The Life of Billie Holiday

Chapter 1   7
A Legend Is Born, but Too Late

Chapter 2   25
The Birth of Billie Holiday

Chapter 3   41
A Troubled Life

Part II: The Works of Billie Holiday

Chapter 4   63
The Songs

Chapter 5   79
The Rollercoaster of Success

Chapter 6   97
Lady Day's Impact

Chronology   116

Holiday's Most Important Works   118

Glossary   119

Further Information   122

Bibliography   124

Index   126

About the Author   128

The Life of Billie Holiday

"I hate straight singing. I have to change a tune to my own way of doing it."

—Billie Holiday

Opposite: Billie Holiday's unique talents as a singer have kept her legacy alive.

CHAPTER ONE

A LEGEND IS BORN, BUT TOO LATE

There are two important things to know about Billie Holiday, and the first is that she was not technically an artist of the Harlem Renaissance. Not the way Bessie Smith, Louis Armstrong, or Duke Ellington were. Though she lived in Harlem during the latter half of the movement, she was too young to have really participated in the era. However, if it weren't for the Renaissance and some of its musical forerunners, Holiday may have never had the career that she did. Her career did not exist in a vacuum. It was very much a continuation of the years—and the careers—that had come immediately before.

The Harlem Renaissance was the name given to the cultural, social, and artistic movement that came out of Harlem between the end of World War I (1918) and the mid-1930s. Harlem had become a cultural center, attracting African-American writers,

Opposite: Holiday emotes into the microphone while performing at the Downbeat Club in New York City, circa 1947.

artists, musicians, photographers, poets, and scholars. Many of these people had come from the South, looking to express their talents and escape the **oppression** of segregation and racism. During this period, Harlem was more than the birthplace of an artistic movement: it was also the center of the "New Negro" movement, in which people of color began demanding equal civil and political rights.

The music of the Harlem Renaissance incorporated jazz and the blues. White people interested in the new musical style flocked to Harlem speakeasies. Through their mutual love of music, interracial socializing was encouraged, though the cultural impact of the Renaissance did little to break down the **Jim Crow laws** that were still enforced around the country. It did, however, reinforce racial pride among African Americans.

It's a shame that Billie Holiday was born too late to have been a true participant in the movement. Taking part in the Harlem Renaissance may have given her a sense of belonging that she seemed to lack for most of her life. Holiday was born into a fractured family under a sense of shame, and she had a far from **conventional** upbringing.

This leads to the second important thing to know about Billie Holiday: much of the information that has endured about her existence, much of what is taken as fact, may very well be fiction. Even her FBI file is thin, jumbled, and inconclusive. Some of the source material about Holiday's life comes from newspapers, magazines, and even video recordings. But some comes from unreliable sources.

One of those unreliable sources is Holiday herself. Although she published an autobiography called *Lady Sings the Blues* in 1956, with the assistance of a cowriter, she later claimed she'd never read it. She embroidered or glossed over many of the details of her life in the book. It presents a melodramatic but sanitized version of her life, especially her early years. Many books about Holiday contain anecdotes collected by a writer named Linda Kuehl, who conducted more than 150 interviews with Holiday's colleagues, friends and peers. However, many of those people were elderly, drunk, or otherwise under the influence when she spoke to them. Over time, the truth—as much as multiple memories can be treated as truth—came out. There is now a certain level of agreement about the sad facts of her early life.

HOLIDAY'S PARENTS

Holiday kicked off her autobiography with the following tale: "Mom and Pop were only a couple of kids when they got married. He was eighteen, she was fifteen and I was three." Unfortunately, that was far from the truth. Perhaps this was what she wanted people to think. Or it could have been that she thought it was better than her reality. Regardless, here are the accepted facts of her childhood, such as it was: her mother, Sarah (better known as Sadie), was nineteen, and her father, Clarence, was only sixteen when Holiday was born. They never did get married.

Sadie, in fact, was also born out of **wedlock**. One writer called Billie Holiday "the **illegitimate** daughter of an illegitimate daughter." That status had a far-reaching negative effect on both women's lives.

Not much is known about Sadie's mother, except that her name was Susie and that she had another daughter, Eva, who was Sadie's half-sister. Both girls were born out of wedlock and from

A Legend Is Born, but Too Late   9

Eleanora Fagan, better known as Billie Holiday, at the age of two

different fathers. It's unclear where Susie lived when Sadie was first born, though it was almost certainly on the wrong side of the tracks in Baltimore. When Sadie was almost two years old, her mother married a man named Harris. The three of them moved to Carroll Street in Baltimore. Sadie's last name became Harris, also. Susie worked almost constantly, and Sadie had very little education. In fact, she was working by the time she was ten years old.

Sadie had very little contact with her father, Charles Fagan. He married another woman named Mattie. Mattie and Charles worked hard to improve their station in life. His wife wanted nothing to do with his **slovenly** relatives, especially once she and Charles moved to a better neighborhood and achieved some respectability. She definitely wanted nothing to do with his illegitimate daughter. Charles himself was rumored to be illegitimate. Although his mother and his supposed father raised him, people often gossiped that his real father was white. This was the background of Holiday's family. It came with a lot of secrets and resentment, and not with much love, closeness, or acceptance.

Sadie was working as a maid for a wealthy white family when she met Clarence Holiday, a teenage aspiring musician. It is unlikely that they had a romance. It is rumored that they met at a dance or a fair or some other social gathering. When Sadie found out she was pregnant, Clarence disappeared. Sadie ended up leaving Baltimore to have the baby, partially to protect her own reputation and partially because her family refused to help. She took what was called a "transportation job," where an African American could have his or her travel paid for if he or she provided services for the white person who bought the ticket. She ended up traveling to Philadelphia. At first she found yet another job working as a maid for a rich white couple, but she was fired when her employers discovered she was pregnant and unmarried. In a rare stroke of luck, Sadie found work at Philadelphia General Hospital. It was mostly scrubbing floors, with some waiting on patients, but in exchange she received free **prenatal** medical care.

EARLY LIFE

Billie Holiday was born on April 7, 1915. The name on her birth certificate was, by most accounts, Eleanora Fagan. Some reports list the spelling of her first name as Eleanor or Elinore, and her last name may have been filled in as Harris. Oddly, Clarence Holiday's name is not included on the form. A waiter named Frank DeViese is named as Eleanora's father on the official document. DeViese had befriended Sadie during her time in Philadelphia and may have been with her at the hospital when Eleanora was born. After that, he disappeared from both Sadie's life and the history books.

Sadie remained in Philadelphia for a time after her daughter was born. Eventually, she called her half-sister Eva to ask her to help with the baby. Eva sent her husband, Robert, to retrieve Eleanora. When they arrived back in Baltimore, she was dropped off with Robert's mother, a total stranger.

Baltimore was not as **cosmopolitan** as its neighbor to the southwest, Washington, DC. Though it falls below the Mason-Dixon Line, Maryland had stayed with the Union during the Civil War. People there still shared many of the Deep South's racist views of African Americans, however. Though Baltimore had some opportunities for poor African Americans in the canning and shipping industries, the neighborhoods where they lived were dirty and overcrowded.

Baby Eleanora lived with Eva and Robert Miller's family for the first three years of her life. Her mother, Sadie, didn't return to Baltimore until 1918. Unfortunately, Eleanora was not treated well by her distant relatives. Sadie's illegitimacy was shameful enough, but now she'd had an illegitimate baby herself. While Holiday's

Holiday grew up on the wrong side of the tracks in Baltimore, Maryland.

A Legend Is Born, but Too Late

autobiography cannot be accepted as absolute truth, she told stories of being punished and treated poorly by her cousins. Her grandfather, Charles Fagan, may have visited occasionally and shown her affection, but her upbringing was far from warm and loving.

When Sadie returned to Baltimore, she too lived with Eva and Robert Miller at first. Then she met and married Philip Gough, a **longshoreman**. She, Eleanora, and Gough moved into their own home. Sadie's father, Charles Fagan, even helped them get the house. For nearly three years, Eleanora and Sadie experienced some stability in their lives, and Eleanora must have felt what it was like to live as part of a family. Then Gough abandoned them and disappeared, and they lost the house. Sadie couldn't keep up with the payments on her meager salary. Her father's wife wouldn't let him support his daughter and granddaughter any more than he already had. Eleanora was sent back to Robert Miller's mother's house. Just like her own mother, Sadie seemed to have little time to parent her child, largely because she was always working or looking for work.

Clarence was not around much, either. He was in the US Army during World War I. When he came back, he started his own career as a jazz guitarist and was often on the road. He was leery of Sadie, afraid that she would lure him into a relationship, or even worse, marriage. He left town for good in 1922—with a new wife.

The instability in Eleanora's home life was not balanced out by the routine of school days. By the time she was in fourth grade, she had skipped school so often that she and her mother were brought to juvenile court. The judge determined that Eleanora

Blues singer Bessie Smith was an early influence on Holiday, who played Smith's records over and over again when she was young.

did not have proper adult care and supervision. He sent her to live at the House of Good Shepherd for Colored Girls, a Catholic institution for wayward girls. It's unclear how long she had to stay there—it was either for ten months or two years. Some accounts say she left after ten months but returned when she was ten or eleven years old after accusing a neighbor of rape. Eleanora told lurid stories about her time in the place. She described **heinous** punishments, girls dying, and being locked in a room with a fellow student's corpse.

When Eleanora got out, Sadie had a new boyfriend. He was a neighborhood troublemaker named Wee Wee Hill. The three of them moved into an apartment in a building that his mother owned. But when Wee Wee wouldn't marry her, Sadie took off for New York City to find better-paying work. She left Eleanora in the care of Wee Wee's mother. Eleanora eventually left Baltimore to join her mother in New York in the late 1920s. She wouldn't return for several years, and when she did, it was as Billie Holiday.

Life in Baltimore wasn't all bad. New Orleans was the birthplace of jazz, and New York City was where it exploded into the public's consciousness and became popular, but Baltimore in the 1920s was also rich with jazz talent. Pianist and composer Eubie Blake, drummer Chick Webb, and bandleader Elmer Snowden—who was friends with Clarence Holiday and played for a time with Duke Ellington—were all products of Baltimore's jazz scene.

Eleanora grew particularly attached to the music of Louis Armstrong and Bessie Smith, which she said she heard while working in a **brothel**. The establishment in question was known as a "good time house," where people got together to talk, drink, and dance. Eleanora's job there is unknown. Some say she was

GLAMOROUS IMAGE

Billie Holiday cared about her appearance when she was performing. She worked in an era where women were expected to be elegant, and female performers were expected to be glamorous. Even when she was traveling the country by bus, she would appear onstage in the most beautiful gown she could afford, with her hair and makeup done. An undated photo of her shows her squeezed into a corner backstage, already wearing a white satin gown and dangling earrings, pinning her hair into place.

Her trademark for many years was a white gardenia in her hair. This started one night when she burned her hair with a curling iron just before she was scheduled to go onstage. Another performer ran down the street to another club and bought a gardenia from the hat-check girl. She then pinned it into Holiday's hair to hide the burned spot. Holiday liked the look of it so much that she decided to continue wearing one. Sometimes the flower was real, but other times it was fabric. Sometimes she attached it up front, above her brow, but most often she wore it cascading along the left side of her face. It added an air of glamour and accentuated her coloring.

In this early publicity photo, Billie is wearing her trademark gardenias in her hair.

working as a prostitute. Some say she was an errand girl for the women who worked there. Either way, she was often heard singing, imitating Smith and Armstrong, so it's safe to say that those two musicians had an influence on her early musical life.

When people heard her sing, they would invite her to sing more. Soon she was spending nights in jazz clubs, jamming with other jazz musicians. This improvisational style served her well in her future. It taught her a lot about the jazz lifestyle. Eleanora may have sung in clubs and speakeasies, even though she was barely in her teens at the time. She looked older, and her talent was unmistakable, which probably helped club owners look the other way.

EARLY INFLUENCES

Louis Armstrong was a New Orleans born-and-bred jazz musician who came to prominence in the 1920s. Known both as Pops and Satchmo, he played the trumpet and sang, splitting much of his time in the 1920s playing for bands in Chicago and New York City. He influenced countless musicians with his unique, innovative trumpet style and his quirky, gravelly vocals. Holiday always said it was his recording of "West End Blues" that made her fall in love with jazz. She was quoted as saying, "I remember Pops' recording of 'West End Blues' and how it used to gas me. It was the first time I ever heard anybody sing without using any words."

She also admitted she copied her rhythmical approach to singing from Armstrong. She imitated his use of **vibrato**, too. While Armstrong would "swing" a single note on his horn, increasing the vibrato just before moving on to a new note, Holiday did the same with her voice. Phil Schaap, curator of Jazz at Lincoln Center, has spent years studying and comparing the two musicians. He can play recordings of the two that show how much of Armstrong's style Holiday learned from listening to his records. It's important to note, though, that Holiday used his style to develop her own unique approach to singing.

Many years later, Holiday would have a professional relationship with Louis Armstrong. They appeared together in the 1947 movie *New Orleans*, in which they portray a couple becoming romantically involved. After that, they became friends who performed and recorded together. They even appeared onstage together at Carnegie Hall in 1947. Unfortunately, there are no recordings of that performance.

On one of Armstrong's own tapes of a 1952 broadcast from Club Hangover, he mentions that Holiday is there in the audience. He then dedicates two songs to her. Best of all, Armstrong and Holiday went into the recording studio once and performed two duets—Armstrong singing, not playing his trumpet. On "You Can't Lose a Broken Heart," Holiday sings first, then Armstrong; they only sing together for four bars. On "My Sweet Hunk o' Trash," the two have a little fun. Holiday's role was to sing about everything that was wrong with Armstrong, while his role was to respond. His responses were mostly ad-libbed. Holiday hardly could have dreamed of such a thing when she was a child, listening to his records in a Baltimore good time house.

Unfortunately, Holiday never recorded with Bessie Smith, who died in a 1937 car accident. When talking about her two early idols, Holiday once said she wanted to "achieve the style of Louis Armstrong and the feeling of Bessie Smith." It was Smith's ability

Holiday clowns around with Louis Armstrong, whose music had a strong influence on her during her childhood.

to awaken emotions with her singing that Holiday loved. Smith, known as the Empress of the Blues, had a distinctive voice that could cut through the noisiest crowd. It was so big and powerful

Bessie Smith in 1936, a year before she died.

that she could fill a room without using a microphone. She, like Holiday, had a commanding stage presence, but Smith was also a comedienne and a natural performer, which Holiday was not. Smith, like Holiday, was a contralto, and she had a range of less than an octave. She had her own style of singing, in which she would pause and take a breath in odd places, or hum, or moan or growl. She cleared the way for other unique singers, like Holiday, although Smith had a much simpler, more straightforward style.

One skill that Holiday probably learned from Smith was clean diction. Smith was a belter, though, and Holiday was not. She admired Smith's big voice and her volume, but she never tried to imitate it. The other major difference between the two may have stemmed from their different ages. Smith sang traditional songs and folksongs, mostly written by African Americans. Holiday's career began at the start of the Tin Pan Alley era, when songs were composed by corporate songwriters, most of whom were white. The two singers had different material and different audiences, though they shared an emotional intensity and the ability to reduce a melody to its barest essentials. Holiday later recorded two of Smith's songs, "St. Louis Blues" and "Gimme a Pigfoot," in her own jazzy style.

Jazz bassist and composer Christian McBride, commenting on Smith's influence on Holiday, said, "I think Billie Holiday has a very large sense of the blues in her voice, and if you listen to Billie Holiday right behind Bessie Smith, you can't help, but go, 'Oh, okay, I hear where she got some of that.' Obviously it's one's own personality flourishing, but you've got to get ideas from somebody."

So began Billie Holiday's life as a jazz musician: self-taught from records she heard at a bordello, and enhanced by her time spent in speakeasies and nightclubs before she was even fourteen years old. She had no idea when she moved to Harlem what would happen next; she just knew that she loved singing.

CHAPTER TWO
THE BIRTH OF BILLIE HOLIDAY

Though Billie Holiday's greatest success and fame came later in the **pantheon** of American jazz, she knew many of the stars of the Harlem Renaissance. She even performed with some of them in their later careers. However, Holiday launched her own career in a different Harlem than the one they had known.

In the early days of the Harlem Renaissance, the population of the Harlem area was about eighty thousand. It had ballooned from a population of fifty thousand in 1910, but it was still a manageable size. By 1930, the population had more than doubled, to nearly two hundred thousand. Harlem had become a city within a city—but a more crowded city. Because of the Great Depression, it had also become a poorer city. There were more people with fewer jobs and less money to go around. Ballrooms, nightclubs, and speakeasies were around during the Renaissance, but by the mid-1920s, drug dens and brothels were popping up as

Opposite: The penitentiary on Welfare Island, where Holiday spent four months after being arrested at the age of fourteen.

well. As Renaissance writer Langston Hughes noted, "We were no longer in vogue, anyway, we Negroes. Sophisticated New Yorkers turned to Noel Coward."

BILLIE HOLIDAY TAKES ON HARLEM

Despite these changes, Harlem was still an exciting place for a young, aspiring performer. Holiday, still known as Eleanora Fagan, remembered seeing limousines driving Harlem's streets, with passengers wearing expensive fur coats. The Cotton Club and the Savoy Ballroom were the hottest spots in town, the Cotton Club for music and the Savoy for dancing. Many dance crazes originated at the Savoy during the 1920s and 1930s. The Savoy would also bring musicians to their stage by hosting a type of battle of the bands. Each band played on a revolving stage at opposite ends of the dance hall. As one band ended a song, the other started playing. The music was constant, and so was the energy and excitement. Eleanora loved it.

However, the glamorous life was not yet hers. When she first moved in with her mother, they lived in a brothel owned by a woman named Florence Williams. It's unclear whether either of them actually worked as a prostitute during this time, but according to police records, shortly after Eleanora moved in the police conducted a raid on the premises. All of the women were brought in for questioning. Eleanora and Sadie both gave false names, and both claimed that Eleanora was twenty-one instead of fourteen. They gave no indication that they were related. Sadie, Florence, and two other women were let go, but Eleanora was sent to the penitentiary on Welfare Island in the East River for four months. It is likely that the judge recognized that Eleanora was younger than twenty-one. This particular judge was known for her mission to clean up the city by ridding the streets of wayward minors.

When Eleanora got out of her first stint in jail, she returned to live with her mother, this time in Brooklyn. After a time, they moved back to Harlem, and she likely got her first singing job. There was a bar called the Grey Dawn cabaret, where she sang with a group called the Hat Hunter Band. She earned whatever money was thrown on the floor at her feet. It may not have been much, but at least she was making a living doing something that she loved. She had vowed that she would never be like her mother, scrubbing floors for white people or selling herself to any man who wanted her.

Eleanora and Sadie moved a lot, which made it difficult to keep a steady singing gig. Then, Sadie found a job at a restaurant, probably in the kitchen, and Eleanora got a job there as a waitress. She would sing in the restaurant to get better tips. Her first break, so to speak, came when she got a gig at a place called Pod's and Jerry's.

Of course, the story of how she got the job has many versions. Here is Holiday's:

> One day, we were so hungry we could barely breathe. I started out the door. It was cold … and I walked from 145th to 133rd … going in every joint to find work … I stopped in the Log Cabin Club run by Jerry Preston … told him I was a dancer. He said to dance. I tried it. He said I stunk. I told him I could sing. He said sing. Over in the corner was an old guy playing the piano. He struck "Trav'lin" and I sang. The customers stopped drinking. They turned around and

watched. The pianist … swung into "Body and Soul." Jeez, you should have seen those people—all of them started crying. Preston came over, shook his head and said, "Kid, you win."

In other accounts, Holiday started to build up a reputation for herself, catching gigs in one club or another. Pod's and Jerry's (also known as the Log Cabin Club or the Catagonia Club) was just one stop on her circuit. However it happened, she began her first engagement there, making two dollars a night plus tips. She sang there every night. By 1933, she had made enough of a name for herself that people started to show up at the club just to hear her sing.

It was at around this time that Eleanora Fagan changed her name to Billie Holiday. The most accepted story is that she chose the name Billie from an actress she admired named Billie Dove. Some researchers also claim that Billie was the natural progression from her father's nickname for her, Bill. However, since she and Clarence spent little time together during her childhood, that's probably a piece of fiction. She decided to use her father's last name, although at first she spelled it Halliday, to differentiate herself from him.

By this time, Clarence was also in New York, playing in Fletcher Henderson's band. He and Billie would sometimes meet up and hang out with other musicians. Billie initially wanted to claim him as her father. However, Clarence didn't want people to know she was his daughter—it made him feel old. He felt that having a daughter cramped his style with the ladies.

Actress Billie Dove

Clarence was far from an ideal father, although the two were now working in the same field. Elmer Snowden claims that the two had a close relationship and that Clarence paternally asked him to watch over Billie while he was on the road. In reality, however, they didn't seem to have much contact outside the clubs. Clarence had a new wife by this point, and she exerted quite a lot of control over him. He also had a white mistress named Atlanta, with whom he had at least two children, so maybe he didn't have much time to be a father to Billie.

When she first moved to New York, Billie had looked up her father. Supposedly, she asked if she could move in with him and his wife, Fanny, but Fanny said no. Fanny hated Sadie. She didn't like to acknowledge that Billie was Clarence's and Sadie's child. Fanny often made rude remarks about Billie's looks, personality, and character. One night when Billie showed up at their house, upset and fearful because Sadie's boyfriend had made a pass at her, Fanny wouldn't let her stay. When Billie got a part-time gig singing with Fletcher Henderson's orchestra, Fanny told Henderson to fire her—probably because Clarence had said that he liked having her there. In fact, Fanny gave Clarence an **ultimatum**: if Billie was allowed to stay with the orchestra, it would mean the end of their marriage, and the breakup wouldn't be pretty.

Pod's and Jerry's was an **integrated** club where "the sporting element," as African Americans with money were called, mixed with rich white people from downtown. This was quite a change from the days of the Harlem Renaissance, when even the infamous Cotton Club was segregated. Pod's and Jerry's was also where Holiday met and first worked with pianist Bobby Henderson, a musician with talent and technique.

Henderson has been described as "a good man and a beautiful pianist" and "the warmest, kindest, gentlest person" many people had ever known. He was totally different from the men that Billie Holiday was usually attracted to, the types that were described as hustlers, pimps, smooth-talkers or rough-talking cats. The two fell in love. One of Henderson's friends said, "Bobby fell like a tree when he met Billie." Henderson himself said, "We had a liking for each other, me and Billie, I never met anybody like her. She was more of a hip woman than I was a hip young man. I was just a square. She was a *woman*, and it surprised me when I knew she was sixteen years old."

Henderson and Holiday were both living with their mothers, and Henderson brought Holiday home to meet his with pride. He wanted his mother to meet "the greatest woman he had ever met in his life." He was enamored of her, of the way she looked, the way she dressed, the way she moved, and even the way she ate. He saw her as graceful, elegant, and almost dainty. Henderson also loved playing for Holiday:

> You could go anywhere and she'd be there, man. Perfect time and perfect diction … I used to play full chords for her. I had a knack, I guess … and I could stay just behind her, so you don't pay no attention to the piano and you just listen to the singer.

Henderson and Holiday eventually broke up, mostly because he knew his personality was not strong enough for her. However, he was present for one of the most important moments in Holiday's early career: her debut at the Apollo Theater. The Apollo seated two thousand people and had two balconies. It was one of the grandest venues in Harlem, and its Amateur Night was famous for launching many careers. Two of Holiday's peers, Ella Fitzgerald and Sarah Vaughan, had gotten their starts at Amateur Night.

Holiday notoriously had opening night stage fright throughout her life, and that night was no exception. While standing backstage, she was so stricken with fear that she couldn't move, and she had to be pushed onstage by comedian Pigmeat Markham. He recalls:

> Billie came on right before the big band closed the show, 'cause that was the big attraction in those days—the big bands … I guess she was tryin' to get her energy to go on stage. She was standing in the wings before she went on; the music comes up; she froze—she just stood there. And I give her a shove—a hard shove and I didn't intend to shove her as hard as I did, and I guess she would have fell, but she grabbed on to the mike and finally she got herself together and she started singin'.

Once she started singing, Holiday relaxed. She performed so well that the audience demanded an **encore**, which rarely happened at the Apollo. She even got invited for a return engagement. She was starting to make a name for herself in New York jazz circles, though it took assistance from a man named John Hammond to start her up the ladder to national and international acclaim and success.

THE POWER OF THE PRESS, AND A PRODUCER

John Hammond saw Billie Holiday perform for the first time in 1933. It's fair to say he was blown away by what he heard. He wrote about it in the international magazine *Melody Maker*:

> This month there has been a real find in the person of a singer named Billie Halliday. Although only eighteen, she weighs over two hundred pounds, is incredibly beautiful, and sings as well as anybody I ever heard.

His comment on her weight and her looks notwithstanding, Hammond's taking notice of Holiday was the turning point of her career.

John Hammond was a **blue blood**, an Ivy League dropout who had likely horrified his parents when he decided to devote his life to music. He was musically trained himself and had already produced some records and published articles exploring the world of African-American music. He had previously launched Count Basie's career when he met Billie Holiday; in later years, he would discover Bob Dylan and Bruce Springsteen. This was a man who could spot talent. Best of all, he had the means to do something about it.

When he first started promoting Holiday, nobody would record her. She wasn't well known outside of certain circles, and she didn't play an instrument. But, as biographer Donald Clarke noted, "Billie was the first singer who was herself a great jazz

John Hammond (*left*), the critic and record producer, discovered and promoted Billie Holiday during the peak years of her career.

musician, as opposed to a musician who also sang." Hammond finally got her into the studio in late 1933. Nothing notable was recorded. The most important thing about these recordings, besides the fact that they were Holiday's first, is that she worked with Benny Goodman. Still a freelance musician at the time, Goodman would have an incredible career himself as a bandleader and the "king of swing." Holiday went back into the recording studio with Goodman and other session musicians a few weeks later. They recorded a Johnny Mercer tune called "Riffin' the Scotch" among a couple of others.

It was her next set of recordings, produced again by Hammond a couple of years later, that really made Holiday's career, reputation, and name as one of jazz's greatest singers. In 1935, Hammond scored a contract for pianist Teddy Wilson, who was known for his dignified playing and elegance. Because everyone was struggling during the Great Depression, Hammond was able to bring in some incredible musicians at low rates. He invited Benny Goodman to play clarinet, although for contractual reasons Goodman played under an assumed name. Also on the roster were saxophonist Ben Webster, who played in the Duke Ellington Orchestra for a time, and a trumpet player named Roy Eldridge. Hammond hired Holiday to do the vocals. Wilson and Holiday rehearsed together ahead of time, and he helped her hone her phrasing and interpretation.

From their first recording of four songs came two hits, "I Wished on the Moon" and "What a Little Moonlight Can Do." Another tune, "Miss Brown to You," stood out as well. The Teddy Wilson small group sessions continued over the next several years and are considered to be among Holiday's best work. Although she was labeled a blues singer by Columbia, only two of the songs were really blues numbers: "Billie's Blues" and "Long Gone Blues." She recorded many compositions by popular songwriters of the day, including "These Foolish Things," "I Can't Give You Anything but Love," "He's Funny That Way," and "The Very Thought of You." She put her personal stamp on show tunes by George Gershwin

SYMPHONY IN BLACK

In 1935, Holiday was cast in a nine-minute movie called *Symphony in Black: A Rhapsody of Negro Life*. The movie was released by Paramount Pictures and starred Duke Ellington as a composer at work. There are no spoken words. Ellington and his orchestra perform the extended composition, using pictures to convey the images running through his mind as he writes *Rhapsody*'s four parts: "The Laborers," "A Triangle," "A Hymn of Sorrow," and "Harlem Rhythm." Holiday appears in the segment called "A Triangle," playing a sad young woman rejected by her man. She performs Ellington's song "The Saddest Tale."

Appearing with Duke Ellington and performing his work was quite an achievement for a twenty-year-old girl who had only started her career the year before. Even more impressive were the glowing reviews of Holiday's performance and dramatic appearance in the film. The whole movie was shot in black and white, and the shadows and light in her segment highlighted her imposing beauty.

The role and her performance also set the tone for her future image of the "I've lost my man and can't get him back, and now I've got the blues" woman.

Holiday rehearses for *Symphony in Black* at the piano with the great Duke Ellington.

and Jerome Kern, including "Summertime" from Gershwin's musical *Porgy and Bess* and Kern's "A Fine Romance" from the movie *Swing Time*. Her versions of "My Man" and "Mean to Me" also came from this time period.

Although these recordings are now considered historic, Holiday only earned a one-time payment each time she worked in the studio. She didn't make royalties or share in any profits.

Jazz pianist Teddy Wilson brought out the best in Holiday. They worked together on some of her finest recordings.

When Teddy Wilson first heard Billie Holiday sing, he was not impressed. He thought she copied Louis Armstrong too closely. He preferred more straightforward, clear-voiced singers. Wilson grew to respect her talent over the years that they worked together, however. He had to admit that the first recording session they did together created magic. "That session was never surpassed," he would say later. "It may have been equaled, but never surpassed." The reason for this was that the musicians treated it almost as a jam session, with the same feelings of energy and collaboration. Holiday was relaxed, and they all enjoyed working together.

No matter what Wilson thought of Holiday's singing, the two were a match made in stylistic heaven. When he played the piano with her, his clean style was a perfect match for Holiday's lean melodies. He learned to match his countermelodies to what she was singing and to fill in between her vocal lines. Playing this way, Wilson enhanced the texture of the song. The only critics who didn't like the two of them together were those who thought jazz still had to be "hot" music—fast, bold, and passionate. Hammond once made a comment, back when Holiday was working with Bobby Henderson, that she always sang better when backed by a good piano player.

If Billie Holiday's career had ended after these recordings, she still would have created some of the best-known and best-loved jazz music in the world. These sessions helped preserve jazz's tradition of small combos at a time when the big band sound was starting to take over the scene. However, her career only grew afterward. Her live performances made as much of an impact on the world as these records—if not more of one. In fact, the big bands were the next challenge she decided to conquer.

HOLIDAY

BELOVED WIFE
BILLIE HOLIDAY
KNOWN AS
LADY DAY
BORN APR 7 1915
DIED JULY 17 1959

DEAR MOTHER
SADIE
1896 — 1945

CHAPTER THREE

A TROUBLED LIFE

It's impossible to write about Billie Holiday without discussing the tragedies in her life as well as the triumphs. She was a woman of stunning ability. Her voice has been called one of the greatest jazz voices of all time, and she influenced many other performers who followed in her footsteps. But all of these accomplishments are paired with the fact that she led a difficult and painful life. Many of her failures played out publicly, and her life ended tragically early.

FAMILY RELATIONSHIPS

Billie Holiday did not come from a loving or supportive family. She ended up having a decent, if tempestuous, relationship with her mother when she reached adulthood. However, Sadie's absence in the earlier years of Holiday's life had to have been painful. When

Opposite: Billie and her mother, Sadie, share a headstone at St. Raymond's cemetery in Brooklyn, New York.

they still lived together, before Holiday left to live with her first husband, the two were known to fight and argue. Bobby Henderson remembers the two of them trying to get him involved in their frequent arguments. He also remembers Holiday confiding in him about how her childhood had been difficult, painful, and isolating.

Holiday had no sisters and brothers—at least none that her father ever told her about. He had two children with his white mistress, but Holiday never met them. In fact, she didn't know they existed until after her father passed away. If he'd had any children with his wife, Fanny, Holiday probably would have been kept away from them. Sadie never had any other children.

Clarence was an absentee father for most of Holiday's life. He only publicly acknowledged her as his daughter much later in his life, when she was starting to become famous. Holiday was able to get a small measure of revenge on him. She once threatened to tell his girlfriend that she was his daughter unless he gave her money.

However, when Clarence died in 1937, it was a blow to Holiday. Things had been looking up in her career. Then she got a call informing her that her father had died while he was on the road in Texas with the Don Redman Orchestra. Holiday was devastated. She blamed his death on the racism of the Deep South. Clarence had been ill, but he avoided seeking medical attention until it was too late. He hadn't wanted to ask for treatment in a rural Texas hospital, where he might have been refused for being black. He wanted to wait until they got to a city, where he'd have a better chance of proper care. His chest cold turned to **pneumonia**, though, and it killed him at the young age of thirty-seven. Holiday was stricken with grief over the circumstances of his death. It also meant that she would never develop a better

HER FAITHFUL COMPANIONS

Maybe because her relationships with her family, boyfriends, and husbands were so unsatisfactory, Holiday kept dogs as pets for several years. The dog that was with her the longest was probably her boxer, Mister. He is featured in many pictures with Holiday, both posed publicity photos and candid snapshots. He accompanied her to shows and hung out in clubs while she was performing. He would wait for her in her dressing room until she was finished singing. Mister has even been immortalized in a book for young children called *Mister and Lady Day: Billie Holiday and the Dog Who Loved Her*.

Later, she had two Chihuahuas named Chiquita and Pepi. Just like the starlets of today, Holiday was often photographed carrying them around—dressed to the nines in sunglasses and fur coats. Chiquita would have her nails done in the same color as Holiday's, and Holiday knitted her little sweaters. Pepi, who was given to her by the actress Ava Gardner, was Holiday's closest companion toward the end of her life. He accompanied her everywhere—to restaurants, church, and even to jail when she was arrested in 1956.

A glamorous Holiday poses for a publicity portrait with her beloved dog, Mister.

relationship with her father. They had shared a bond over being musicians, and maybe that's all she would have gotten from him had he lived, but she still mourned the lost opportunity. Holiday was also shocked to discover, at his funeral, that she had a half-sister and a half-brother, courtesy of his longtime mistress, Atlanta.

Sadie died eight years later. Her death wasn't as abrupt—she had been ill for months and suffered a stroke—but it was still a shock for Holiday when she got the news. This time, she was the one on the road, touring with Joe Guy's band, so she hadn't been with her mother at the end of her life, either.

The mother and daughter had a complicated relationship. They struggled through poverty together, often making bad choices, but it brought them closer to each other. Holiday appreciated her mother's good qualities, like her generosity, warmth, and humor, so she was distraught at losing her. Holiday felt guilty for not being with her mother when she was dying, and for leaving her in the first place. She regretted not sending money. She fretted that she was going to be judged by God and sent to hell—her Catholic upbringing peeking through. Holiday was also inconsolable at having become an orphan, even though she had never really been parented. Holiday never recovered from the guilt and grief she felt after Sadie's death. From this point on, alcohol and drugs played a larger role in Holiday's life.

ILLEGAL SUBSTANCES AND LEGAL WOES

Unfortunately, Billie Holiday became almost as famous for her drug problems as she did for her singing. She herself would have admitted that she was a cautionary tale about the evils of drugs and the ease with which you can get hooked.

Most people, including her friends and her mother, blame Holiday's first husband for starting her on the path to addiction. Jimmy Monroe was handsome and worldly, but he was also a drug dealer and possibly a pimp. He had a dark side and was openly abusive to Holiday even early on in their relationship. He also had a mistress and a drug habit, neither of which he was willing to give up. He was the one who gave Holiday opium and heroin for the first time.

Opium and heroin are both highly addictive narcotics. Although Holiday may not have known that when she first started taking them, she soon learned it. She once said about heroin that "it can fix you so you can't play nothing or sing nothing."

After her marriage to Jimmy ended abruptly—he decided to stay in California after accompanying her there for a gig—Holiday continued to have relationships that were based on drugs. Her next boyfriend, Joe Guy, was also a supplier. Her heroin habit got so bad that she lost weight, damaged her good looks, and started missing gigs. She was also blowing most of the money she made to buy drugs.

In 1946, Holiday's manager encouraged her to go into the hospital to try and kick her drug habit. However, the hospital didn't really know how to treat drug addicts. They didn't deal with any of the sources of Holiday's problem. They didn't give her any kind of counseling, and didn't do much to help her physically, either. Their treatment was to flush her veins with glucose solution and force her go off the drug **cold turkey.**

In addition, although her hospital visit was supposed to be a secret, somebody leaked it to the press. Once the press knew why she was in the hospital, the federal authorities were also clued in to her drug use. The Narcotics Bureau was put on notice. They actually had her tailed for a year after she got out, all across the country.

With this lack of appropriate treatment, Holiday failed to kick her drug addiction. She was arrested for possession of narcotics not a year later. Her boyfriend and another man were arrested along with her. The men were both released on technicalities, but Holiday was sentenced to a year in prison. Worse, the prison was in the southern state of West Virginia, and it was segregated. Holiday was forced to go through withdrawal cold turkey again,

Accompanied by her pianist, Bobby Tucker, Billie Holiday is charged with heroin possession in Philadelphia, Pennsylvania.

A Troubled Life 47

and she had to do chores. Cleaning, hauling coal, and slopping pigs were a far cry from her glamorous life on the stage. She wasn't allowed to receive any of the letters and gifts sent to her from friends and fans around the world, so she had no emotional or moral support. She refused to sing while she was there, and she never got over her sense of shame over being imprisoned.

Drug-related problems plagued Holiday for the rest of her life. One club owner, John Levy, was so angry when she tried to quit singing for him that he had her arrested on a phony drug charge. Once again, her arrest was highly publicized. At least this time she was able to get the charges dropped.

Her heroin use caused her to lose friends, bookings, and recording contracts. She got high during a concert at Carnegie Hall in the early 1950s and had to be helped off stage. Finally, she was arrested again in 1956, for heroin possession, while staying in Philadelphia.

Holiday added alcohol to her list of addictions by the mid-1950s. It may have been that when she was trying to cut down on her heroin use. She drank hard liquor instead. She developed cirrhosis of the liver, a common condition among alcoholics.

In late May 1959, Billie Holiday collapsed in her apartment and was rushed to the hospital. There she was diagnosed with cirrhosis and heart failure. She was admitted to the hospital in critical condition. Yet, someone was still bringing her drugs. A nurse found an envelope of white powder in Holiday's room and alerted the authorities. The police came to the hospital and placed her under arrest. They took her mug shot and fingerprints while she was lying in bed. They also kept her under guard because she was unable to attend trial. Never mind that she was unable to get out of bed or do much at this point.

Billie Holiday died in that hospital on July 17, at the age of forty-four. The official cause of death was congestion of the lungs compounded by heart failure. Her heavy use and abuse of alcohol and drugs certainly played a large part in her death.

Crowds gathered to watch as Billie Holiday's coffin was carried into St. Paul the Apostle church in New York City.

PROFESSIONAL FALLOUT

The biggest problem Holiday faced after her yearlong stint in jail was losing her ability to sing in New York clubs. In those days, in order to perform anywhere that sold liquor, singers and musicians had to possess a cabaret card. The New York City police gave performers these permits. Because Holiday was a convicted criminal, her cabaret card was revoked. She could no longer sing in nightclubs or bars in New York City unless the gig lasted less than four days. She had lost her main source of revenue in the city where she lived. Holiday had to travel to other cities to secure long-term engagements. She called herself a "DP," a displaced person, which was the term used for refugees after World War II.

Holiday suffered emotionally, also. She worried that people only came to her concerts to check for track marks on her arms or to see if she was high or unable to perform. And, of course, some people refused to book her at all because she was now a known drug addict. In 1957, CBS was putting together a special called "The Sound of Jazz," and they planned to have Holiday appear. Some sponsors protested, saying "We must not put into America's homes, especially on Sunday, someone who's been imprisoned for drug use." Luckily, several other people involved with the show threatened to quit if Holiday was removed from the lineup.

In 1953, Holiday was invited to appear on an ABC show called *The Comeback Story*. It was somewhat like a modern reality show. Hosted by George Jessel, the program featured people who had overcome hardships in their lives. Holiday discussed her addiction, poverty, and the racism she had experienced in her career.

RACISM

Being an African-American celebrity in Billie Holiday's era meant being two people: the glamorous star on the stage and the person who had to live in the real world. Living in the real world meant living with racism, prejudice, and segregation. One of the most ridiculous experiences Holiday suffered was during her time with the Count Basie Orchestra. She was on the road with them, and while they were playing in Detroit, the venue's manager told her to darken her light skin with makeup. Otherwise, he said, she might be mistaken for a white woman. He believed it would upset the audience too much to see a white woman performing onstage with black musicians. Holiday claims this was the reason she quit working with Basie. As always, however, there are several versions of the story, and sources disagree about the reason the two stopped working together.

Next, Holiday signed on to perform on tour with Artie Shaw and his orchestra. All of the musicians in his band were white—as was Shaw, who thought he was prepared to handle any racist incidents that might occur. When the band toured the South, however, Holiday was unable to get food or service at any restaurants with the rest of the band. She wasn't allowed to stay in the same hotels as the band—if she could get a hotel room at all. On at least one occasion she was in pain for months because she couldn't find adequate medical care due to her race. She was called racial slurs to her face, both in public places and when she was onstage. Her bandmates tried hard to support her, but there was little they could do.

Billie Holiday

Holiday performed with Count Basie and his orchestra many times over the years.

A Troubled Life

Count Basie's management had tried to avoid some of these problems by renting temporary apartments for the band whenever possible. That way, they wouldn't have to worry about being turned away by hotels, and they could cook their own meals. Some of the band members later reminisced about Holiday's good cooking.

As hard as it was to be treated poorly in the South, Holiday said she preferred upfront racism to the North's hypocrisy. The North was supposed to be more enlightened about racism, but that's not what she experienced.

When the band returned to New York City, they got a gig at a hotel from which a radio show was broadcast. It was supposed to be a big break for Shaw, and it would have been a big break for Holiday, too. However, the show's sponsors didn't want an African-American singer featured prominently on the show. They told Shaw to limit Holiday to one or two songs during the one-hour broadcast. She also had to stay in her dressing room when she was not performing. On top of that, the hotel manager refused to allow her to sit in the hotel bar or restaurant or mingle with the guests in any way. He told her she had to use the kitchen entrance to the hotel, not the front door, and would need to use the freight elevator, not the one the guests used. Shaw tried to go to bat for her, but faced with the threat of losing the gig, he backed down. Holiday quit soon after. She swore off singing with dance bands because though swing bands had started out with black musicians, they were now being replaced with white bands. The white bands were taking over and making all the money.

Once, in the late 1930s, Holiday got a gig out in Hollywood, California. She was appearing at a club and hobnobbing with movie stars. She spent her time there hanging out with Bob Hope, who once defended her against a heckler in the audience, and Clark

Gable, who once fixed her car. Then the club closed suddenly. Holiday didn't receive her paycheck, and she had to take a bus all the way back to New York. To add insult to injury, she had to sit in the back of the bus when it passed through certain states because of the Jim Crow laws that were still in effect.

Much later in her career, Holiday agreed to go on a tour through the Southern states with Gerald Wilson and his band. For that tour, they called themselves the Lady Day Orchestra. They painted that name on the tour bus, which took them from

Jim Crow laws in action at a bus station in North Carolina, 1940

A Troubled Life

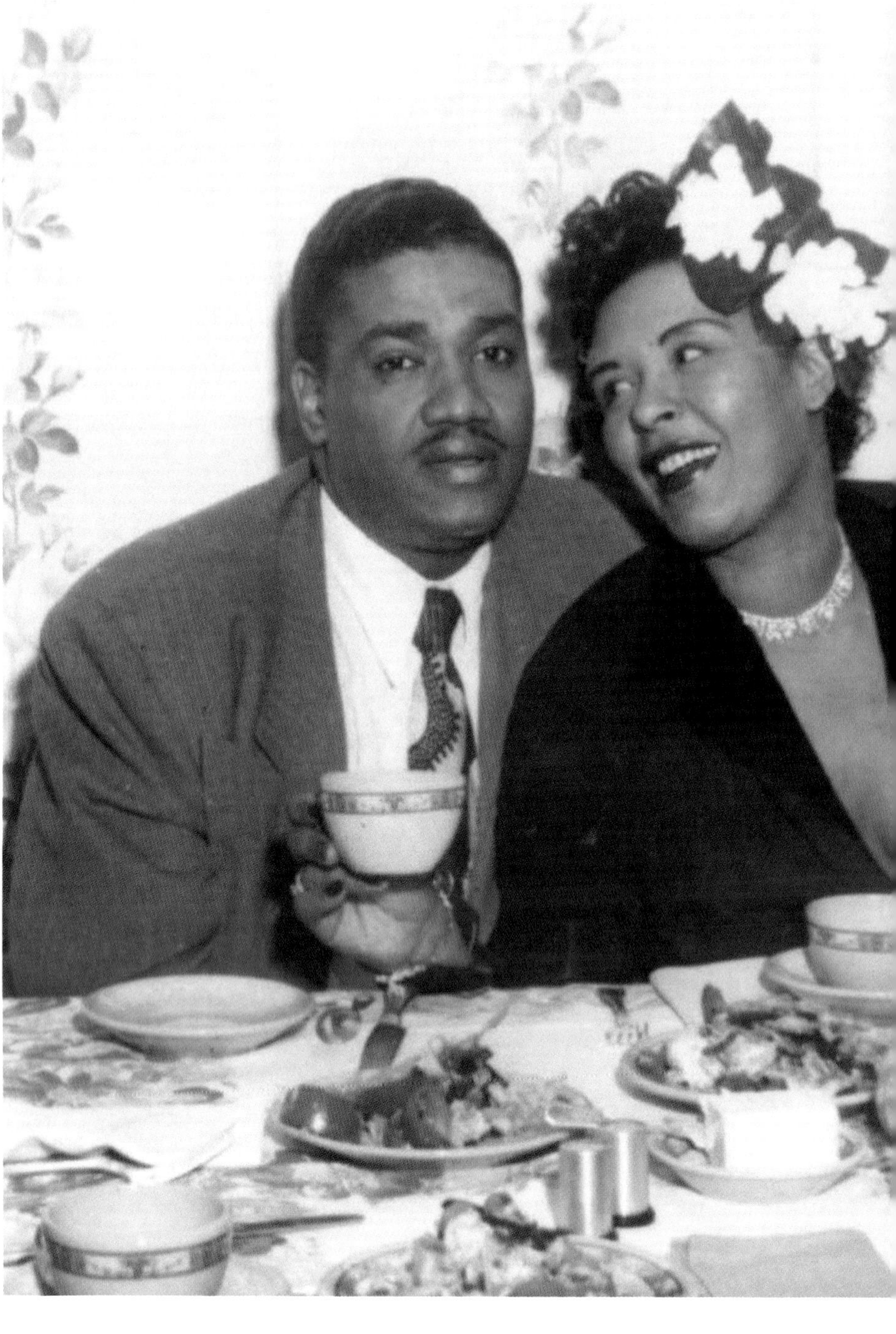

Holiday with her second husband, Louis McKay

A Troubled Life **57**

show to show. Holiday had avoided the Southern states ever since her bad experiences with the Count Basie and Artie Shaw orchestras. Perhaps she thought things would be better in 1950. Unfortunately, the tour was badly planned and mismanaged from the start. Despite all their hard work, there was no money coming in.

Somewhere in the Carolinas, the bus driver announced he was fed up with the situation, and he walked out on them. The entire band was stranded on a Southern highway. John Levy, who was Holiday's manager at the time, said he was going to go find some money, and he disappeared also. Holiday supposedly went with him. The rest of the band was left there with no money and nowhere to sleep except on the bus. The bus driver was the only white person on the tour with them. They had needed a white person in the group; in towns where restaurants refused to serve African Americans, he could always go in and order sandwiches for everyone. He could also get service at gas stations.

Every night after they were abandoned on the bus, a group of policemen came up to the bus and hit it with their nightsticks. They told the black musicians that "if anything went wrong in the town," they would be held responsible. This was the world that Billie Holiday was still living in, decades into her career.

MARRIAGES

Holiday was married twice. Neither time was for love. If anyone was getting married for money, though, it was her spouses.

Her first husband, Jimmy Monroe, abandoned the relationship after less than a year. He accompanied Holiday on her trip to California. When the club closed and Holiday was forced to return home, Monroe told her he was staying. He'd made connections with some drug smugglers, and he decided to explore the possibilities. Holiday didn't divorce him for years, and she even bailed him out when he was arrested for smuggling. She gave him money for a lawyer, which was never returned because he was convicted and sent to jail.

Holiday only married her second husband, Louis McKay, for legal reasons. They had both been arrested for narcotics possession. If they were married, she wouldn't have to testify against him— nor he against her. She obtained a quickie divorce from Monroe, sixteen years after he left her, and married McKay. Though she and McKay were separated at the time of her death, that didn't stop him from attempting to control her estate. He raised the ire of her fans when they discovered that he had neglected to put up a headstone at her grave. He eventually remedied the situation, but it was obvious that he cared little for Holiday once she was no longer providing for him.

PART II

The Works of Billie Holiday

"You can't copy anybody and end with anything. If you copy, it means you're working without any real feeling. No two people on earth are alike, and it's got to be that way in music or it isn't music."

—Billie Holiday

Opposite: Holiday in 1943, before her troubles started

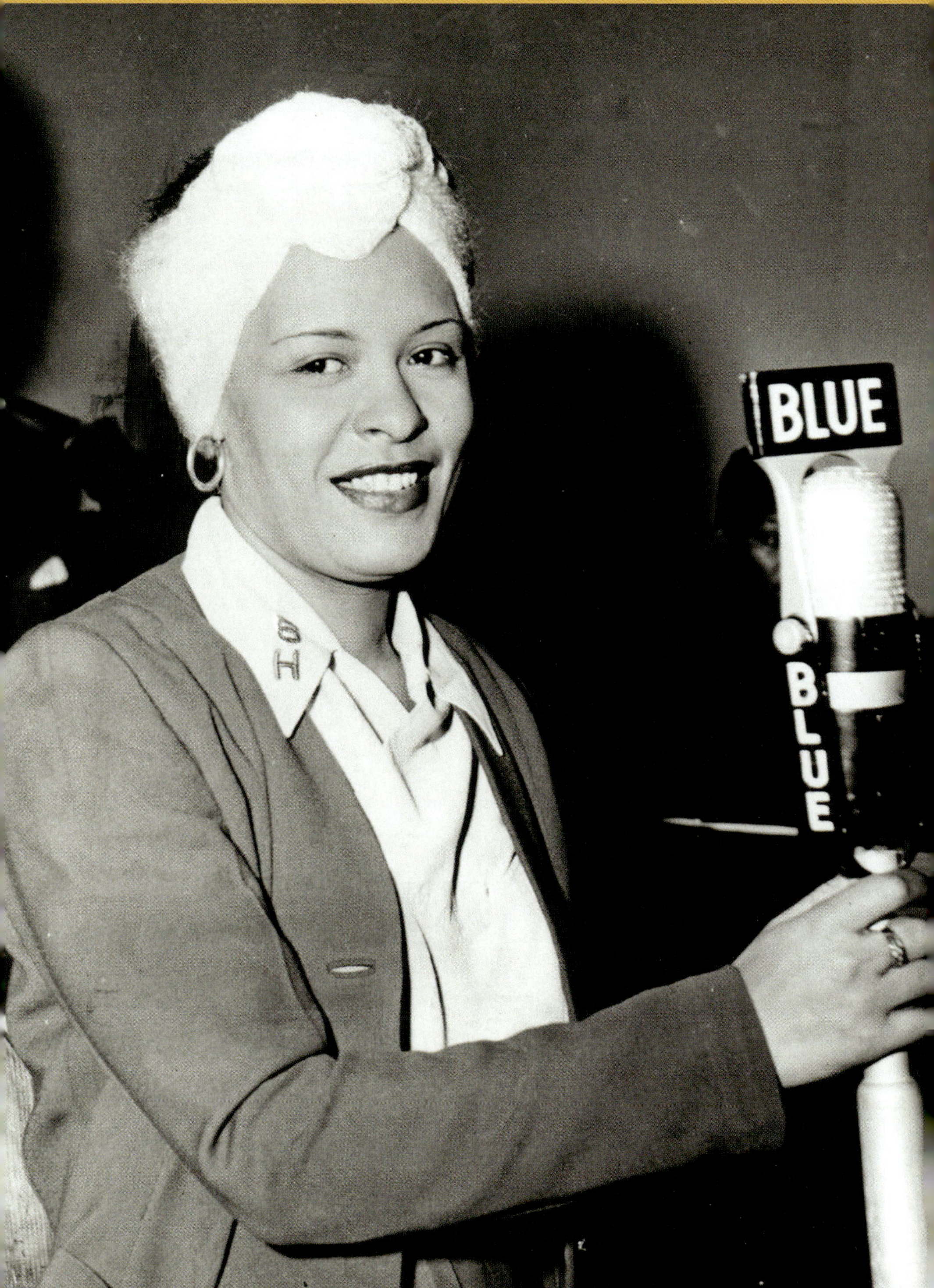
BLUE
BLUE

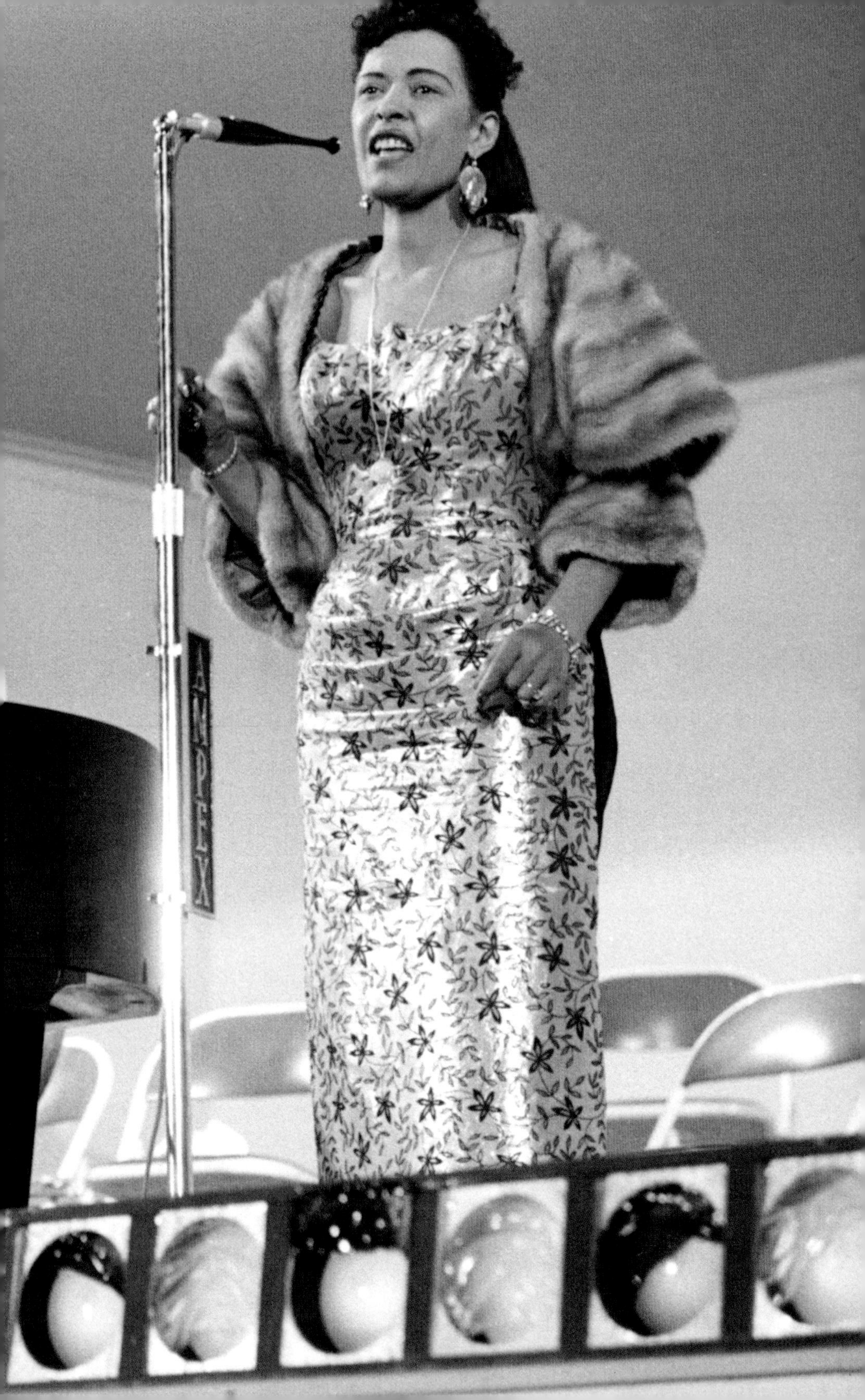
AMPEX

CHAPTER FOUR

THE SONGS

Billie Holiday performed innumerable tunes throughout her career, but there are several that immediately bring her to mind. "When a Woman Loves a Man," "What a Little Moonlight Can Do," "Gloomy Sunday," and "Mean to Me" are among the most popular songs in her repertoire. "'Tain't Nobody's Business If I Do," a defiant song of individual choice and ill-advised loyalty, could have been written about the later years of her life, especially.

The recordings she made while working with producer John Hammond between 1935 and 1939 are considered to be the peak of her career. Backed by pianist Teddy Wilson and other outstanding musicians, the records include her renditions of "These Foolish Things," "I Can't Give You Anything But Love," "He's Funny That Way," and a handful of Gershwin and Kern show tunes. Her versions of "What a Little Moonlight Can Do,"

Opposite: Holiday performed at the Monterey Jazz Festival in 1958, less than a year before her death.

"My Man," and "Mean to Me" are also well known. One song, which she cowrote, was called "Billie's Blues" and seemed to be a reflection of her by-then established image of a woman done wrong by a man. The song starts with the lyrics:

> Lord I love my man, tell the world I do
> I love my man, tell the world I do
> But when he mistreats me
> Makes me feel so blue

Even among all these great recordings, there are three songs that particularly stand out. No matter who wrote them or who else sang them, these three songs are the ones that are most associated with Billie Holiday and her unique vocalizations and interpretations. They're the ones that people will mention when they hear her name, and for good reason.

"GOD BLESS THE CHILD"

This song has become a staple in modern culture. It's been used in movies, from the Holocaust drama *Schindler's List* to the comedy *Two Weeks Notice*. Singer-actress Liza Minnelli has performed it in concert for years, as did her mother, Judy Garland. It's been sung on television shows like *Grey's Anatomy*, covered by artists from Tony Bennett to Annie Lennox, and even sampled by rappers and hip-hop artists.

Holiday originally recorded it in 1941, backed by Eddie Heywood and His Orchestra. She later released a different version in 1956 on her album *Lady in Autumn*. While she is given songwriting credit for it, along with collaborator Arthur Herzog Jr., there is some controversy about this. Holiday first claimed the song was about a fight she had with her mother over money. Sadie had asked Holiday to help fund a little after-hours joint she

The sheet music for "God Bless the Child," one of Holiday's biggest hits

The Songs 65

wanted to open. Holiday said that when she turned her mother down, the two got into an argument, and her mother said the line "God bless the child that's got his own." After stewing with anger over the fight for three weeks, Holiday said the song just "fell into place in my head." A similar version of the story reverses one point, claiming it was Sadie who turned down Holiday for a loan, and Holiday who snapped back with the retort. She then took this supposedly whole song to Herzog, who made a tweak or two, and the song was done. Holiday also claimed some of the lyrics were based on passages from the Bible—but nobody has ever figured out which passages she could have meant.

Herzog remembered the story far differently. In his version, he went to Holiday and asked for her help in writing a new song. At the time, NBC and CBS were boycotting the American Society of Composers, Authors and Publishers (ASCAP) because ASCAP was demanding higher royalty rates for music played on the radio. For ten months, radio stations couldn't play any songs by artists that ASCAP represented. Herzog saw it as an opportunity to get new songs not registered with ASCAP into heavy rotation. He said he asked Holiday for "an old-fashioned Southern expression" that he could base a song on. She gave him the phrase, that became the song's title. Herzog swore he wrote the song, both words and music, in twenty minutes. Holiday, he said, made only one contribution beyond the title: asking him to move one note down half a step. This version of the story is also doubtful. Holiday wasn't Southern, really, and although she had been raised Catholic, she wasn't particularly religious.

Even the title may be wrong. The song is supposedly about the disparity between people who have money or things, and those who don't. The repeated lyric of the song goes:

*Mama may have, Papa may have
But God bless the child that's got his own.*

Why is God blessing a child that has his own money? What makes more sense is the theory that the original title of the song, or the proverb that it was supposedly based on, was "God *Blessed* the Child"—because the child who has his own doesn't need to rely on anyone else.

No matter who wrote it or where the inspiration came from—although it should be noted that John Hammond backed Herzog's version of the story—Holiday's version of "God Bless the Child" was honored with the Grammy Hall of Fame Award in 1976. It was also included in the list of Songs of the Century by the Recording Industry Association of America and the National Endowment for the Arts.

"LOVER MAN"

Holiday had been singing this song in the clubs for years when producer Milt Gabler decided she should record it. Holiday had wanted to record a tune while backed by an orchestra, and Gabler agreed. He said this would be the right song for her idea. Jazz singers weren't usually accompanied by string instruments, so this was a move toward a more popular sound. Some of her fans and critics were unhappy that she took this new approach. No matter. Billie Holiday became the first African-American artist in her field to record with strings. The results have been described as magical.

This recording was also significant because it was the first time Holiday received royalties on the sale of one of her records.

Holiday's music is still popular today.

However, this was another song whose authorship is unclear. According to Holiday, Jimmy Davis wrote the song for her in 1942. She downplayed the contributions of the other credited authors, Roger Ramirez and James Sherman. On the song's official registered version, however, Ramirez is listed as the composer, and Davis and Sherman are named as the songwriters.

"Lover Man" became Billie Holiday's only major chart success, despite its racy lyrics. Even Ramirez was shocked that it was recorded, let alone released, because of the suggestiveness of the words.

> I go to bed with a prayer
> That you'll make love to me
> Strange as it seems
>
> Someday we'll meet
> And you'll dry all my tears
> Then whisper sweet
> Little things in my ear
> Hugging and a-kissing
> Oh, what I've been missing
> Lover man, oh, where can you be?

The song climbed to the number five spot on the R&B charts in 1945 and made it into the top twenty of the pop charts as well. Backed by Toots Camerata and His Orchestra, the melody alternates between minor and major keys, while Holiday sings the lyrics slowly, with an air of dejection. The lyrics start with the line "I don't know why I'm feeling so sad," a lonely perspective that everyone can identify with. They end with the last rendition of the question, "Oh lover man, where can you be?" Again, in this song, Holiday portrays a lost, lonely, and heartbroken woman.

"STRANGE FRUIT"

This song was aptly named. It was a strange choice for Billie Holiday, and it sticks out of her repertoire like the proverbial sore thumb. "Strange Fruit" is not a romantic song, nor a love-gone-wrong song. It's a song about **lynching**. The images it paints are of bodies burning and rotting, faces distorted in death, and blood spattered on the leaves beneath a tree where a hanging has taken place. The "strange fruit" of the title refers to the bodies of black men who have been hung from tree branches.

The song was written not by an African-American activist or civil rights leader. It was by a white Jewish high school teacher from the Bronx. Abel Meeropol was his name, and he'd been shaken by a photograph he'd seen of a lynching. He was especially disturbed by the reactions of the people who were standing by when it had happened.

Contemporary musician Marcus Miller, who has recorded his own version of the song, points out that it took tremendous courage both for Meeropol to write the song and for Holiday to sing it. "The '60s hadn't happened yet," he explains. "Things like that weren't talked about. They certainly weren't sung about." When Miller says the '60s hadn't happened yet, he's referring to the civil rights movement. In fact, the civil rights movement wouldn't start for another fifteen years. Protest songs didn't become popular until the 1950s.

Also, Holiday was not what she or anyone else would call political. Although she had certainly faced racism herself and almost certainly knew people who had witnessed lynchings, that type of violence was not part of her personal experience. For a jazz and pop artist to agree to sing such a controversial song was unusual. It became a noteworthy leap in her career. Part of the reason for this is the way she sang it, but it's not as if she was eager to do so at first. The lyrics were so grim, and she was afraid of how her public would react.

So, how did a rising jazz star come to record a poem written by a public high school teacher? The floorshow director at Café Society, Robert Gordon, heard it performed at an anti-**fascist** fundraiser (Meeropol was a **communist**). Gordon sought out Meeropol and told him to bring the song to Barney Josephson.

Holiday poured out her heart and soul when she was singing.

The Songs

Josephson was the owner of Café Society, where Billie had just started a long-term contract. Josephson was quoted later as saying he didn't really know what to do with the song. He was floored by the lyrics, but also offput. Nevertheless, he agreed to let Meeropol present it to Holiday. Although at first he thought she was unenthusiastic or possibly didn't understand the song—which of course she did—she agreed to perform it.

The first time Holiday sang the song at Café Society, it seemed like her first instinct was correct:

> The first time I sang it, I thought it was a mistake ... There wasn't even a patter of applause when I finished. Then a lone person began clapping nervously. Then suddenly everyone was clapping.

Jack Schiffman, a member of the family that ran the Apollo Theater, remembers a similar, stunned reaction from the audience when Holiday sang it for the first time on that stage:

> When she wrenched the final words from her lips, there was not a soul in that audience, black or white, who did not feel half strangled ... A moment of oppressively heavy silence followed, and then a kind of rustling sound I had never heard before. It was the sound of almost two thousand people sighing.

To amplify the drama of the song, Josephson had Holiday perform it as the last song of every set, three sets a night. When it came time for her to sing it, the lights in the restaurant all went down. It would be pitch black. The waiters would cease serving, and Holiday would stand perfectly still on stage. Just a pinpoint spotlight illuminated her face as she sang. Often, she would cry while singing it, although the tears never interfered with her voice. As she sang the last line, the lights would go completely out. When they came back up, she would be gone from the stage and would not return for an encore. Sometimes, customers would be so overcome, they would get up and leave. Once, a woman confronted Holiday in the ladies room later that night, screaming at her never to sing that song again. The woman had once witnessed a lynching as a little girl, and it had traumatized her. She certainly never expected to be reminded of it during a night on the town.

Holiday received a lot of attention for "Strange Fruit," and not all of it was positive. *Variety* magazine called it "a depressing piece." Her mother hated it and questioned why she would sing it. A reviewer in *Down Beat* magazine complained, "Perhaps I expected too much of 'Strange Fruit,' the ballyhooed … tune which, via gory wordage and hardly any melody, expounds an anti-lynching campaign … At least, I'm sure it's not for Billie." Her former producer and onetime greatest promoter, John Hammond, criticized it, saying it was artistically the worst thing she could have done. He called it the beginning of the end of her career. In later years, some nightclub owners refused to let her sing it. She eventually had to have it written into her contract that she be allowed to perform it. Although she claimed singing it made her sick, she performed it for the rest of her career, across both the United States and Europe. She was proud of the effect it had on people. However, Holiday also believed that the song brought her to the attention of the Federal Bureau of Narcotics and the FBI, both of whom she ran into trouble with later.

Billie Holiday

Holiday sings during a recording session in 1939.

The Songs

When it came time to record the song, there was still more controversy. Columbia Records, where Holiday then had a contract, refused to do it. They cited fear of antagonizing Southern customers. Milt Gabler, owner of Commodore Records, believed in the song. He went to Columbia and asked them for permission to borrow Holiday for a recording session. She and the musicians he hired for the day created two records, one with "Strange Fruit" on the A side and "Fine and Mellow" on the B side. Although some stations banned the record in the United States and England, it sold ten thousand copies in its first week and peaked at number sixteen on the charts. Not bad for a song that *Time* magazine dismissed as "a prime piece of musical propaganda" for the NAACP. The *Time* magazine writer also criticized Holiday's weight in his article, so the review should be taken with a grain of salt. The *New York Times* was much more respectful. Their reviewer said, "[It] makes you blink and hold to your chair. Even now, as I think of it, the short hair on the back of my neck tightens, and I want to hit somebody."

Copies of the record were sent to all members of the US Senate as a form of protest against lynching. Civil rights activists congratulated Holiday on performing and recording the song. Music journalist Leonard Feather defined "Strange Fruit" as "the first significant protest in words and music, the first unmuted cry against racism," while record producer Ahmet Ertegun once called it "a declaration of war ... the beginning of the civil rights movement." Fellow singer Lena Horne said Holiday "was putting into words what so many people had seen and lived through. She seemed to be performing in melody and words the same things I was feeling in my heart." Drummer Max Roach perhaps summed it up best when he said, "She made a statement that we all felt as black folks.

No one was speaking out. She became one of the fighters, this beautiful lady who could sing and make you feel things."

"Strange Fruit" defies easy musical categorization. As author David Margolick, who wrote an entire book about the song, explains, "It is too artsy to be folk music, too explicitly political and polemical to be jazz." He adds that "no song in American history has ever been so guaranteed to silence an audience or to generate such discomfort." Joe Segal, who has run the second-oldest jazz club in America for fifty years, would agree. He said he can't listen to the song when it comes on the radio: "It's too stark. I can't handle it."

Despite the many controversies that surround the song, the Library of Congress added "Strange Fruit" to the National Recording Registry in 2002. The *Atlanta Journal-Constitution* slotted the song at number one on their list of "100 Songs of the South." The Recording Industry Association of America, the National Endowment for the Arts, and Scholastic added it to their "Songs of the Century" list. This list is part of an education project that was started to "promote a better understanding of America's musical and cultural heritage" in American schools. Finally, although the publication had panned it sixty years earlier, *Time* magazine called "Strange Fruit" the song of the century in 1999.

In the years since Holiday's death, many other artists have recorded their own versions of "Strange Fruit." Among these musicians are Carmen McRae, Lou Rawls, Nina Simone, Diana Ross, UB40, Sting, Siouxsie and the Banshees, Tori Amos, and Cassandra Wilson. Yet, the song was so personal to her, and her interpretation was so riveting, that some people would prefer that nobody else touch it. Dan Morgenstern, director of the Institute of Jazz Studies at Rutgers, has said, "Frankly, I don't think anybody but Billie should do it. I don't think anybody can improve on it."

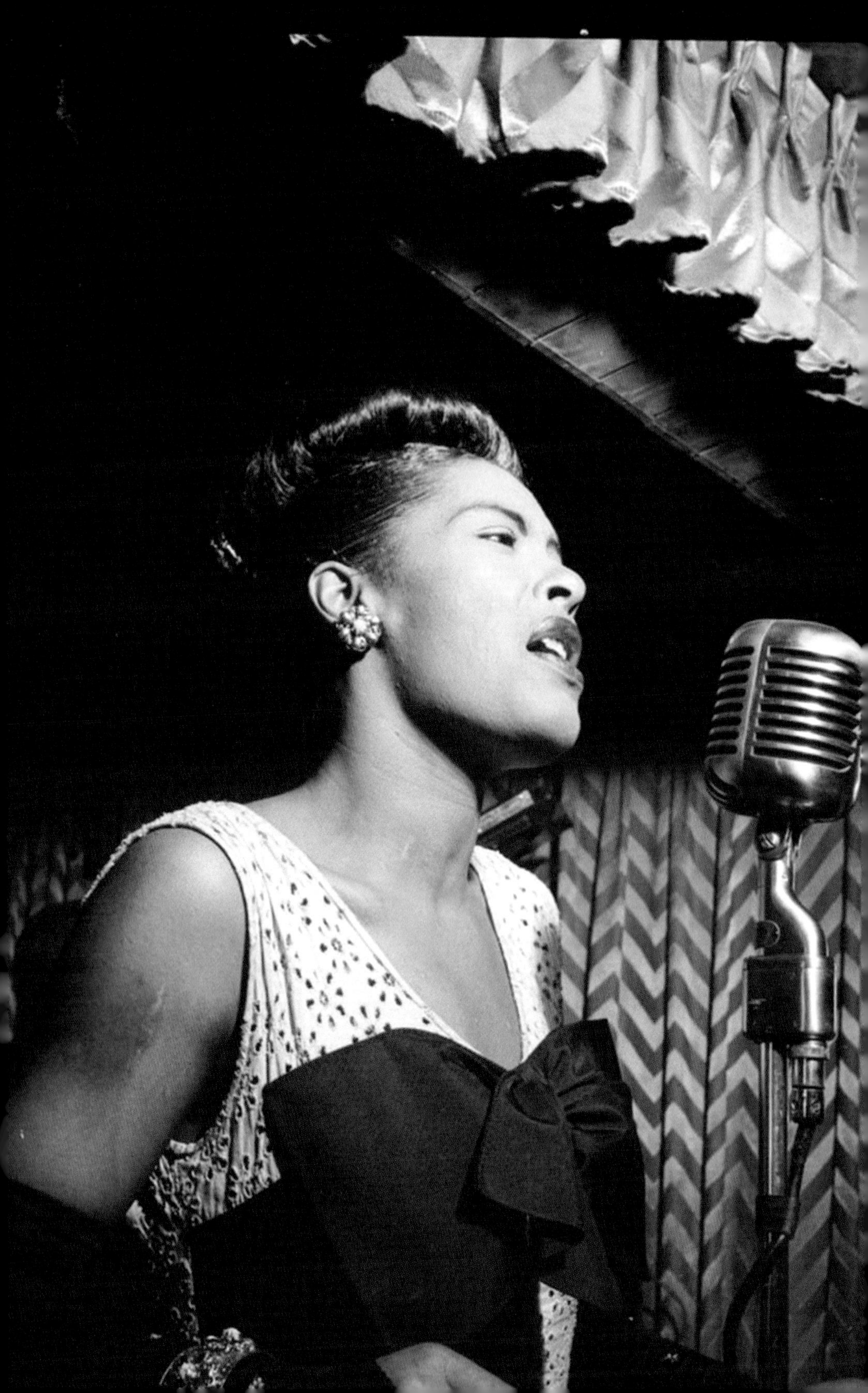

CHAPTER FIVE
THE ROLLERCOASTER OF SUCCESS

Love it or hate it, Billie Holiday's voice is what set her apart from other singers. Her vocal style, her tone, and her phrasing are what people focus on when they listen to her sing. These features are what engender the strong emotions and opinions that people express over her. They are also the reasons her work has endured over the last several decades.

Holiday's predecessors like Bessie Smith, Ma Rainey, and Dinah Washington were all strong performers in their own right, but they were blues singers. As much as Holiday might have said that she idolized Smith, Holiday was the one who transformed and popularized the art of jazz singing.

With such a spectacular and unique talent, and with the acclaim that she received during her lifetime, it's hard to believe she died almost broke. The story goes that when Holiday passed away in

Opposite: A glamorous portrait of the singer in action, 1947

a New York City hospital, her life savings were found strapped to her leg. The grand total was $750. She supposedly had less than a dollar in her bank account.

EARLY CAREER

The other amazing thing about Billie Holiday's legacy is that over the course of her twenty-five years of public performances, her career went through three distinct periods, and she triumphed in all of them. She may have begun a fourth phase or even a fifth if hard living hadn't damaged her voice and taken her life.

The first period, or "The Hammond Years," fell between 1933 and 1942. Music reporter John Hammond was trying to launch his career as a music promoter and producer. When he saw a seventeen-year-old Holiday performing at a club called Covan's, he was transfixed. He later said, "The way she sang around a melody, her uncanny harmonic sense and her sense of lyric content was almost unbelievable in a girl of seventeen."

He was so impressed by what he saw and heard that he wrote about Holiday immediately. He brought musician friends to her performances and started working to get her a recording contract. Two of the people he brought to hear her sing were Benny Goodman and Joe Glaser, who was Louis Armstrong's manager. Glaser would later take her on as a client, and Benny Goodman agreed to back her on her first recording session.

Holiday's first recording was fairly unmemorable. She was nervous, and the song she sang, "Your Mother's Son-in-Law" was not in a key she found comfortable. When she went in a second time, she recorded a ditty called "Riffin' the Scotch," which had been written with her in mind. It also may have kicked off her career-long theme of a woman who was unlucky in love.

The recordings didn't sell many copies. They did, however, establish Holiday as a professional who could hold her own with first-class musicians. In the meantime, she kept working, booking as many club dates as possible. There was one critic, Marcus Wright of *New York Age*, who panned her, but that was probably because she had insulted him. Audiences loved her.

Then a new face started to appear on the circuit, another young jazz singer named Ella Fitzgerald. Holiday started to worry that she was never going to get her big break, and that Fitzgerald, who had a wide range and a more traditional style, would overtake her. That was when John Hammond got her back into the studio with Teddy Wilson, and she made the recordings that made her famous. These were done in the new swing style, and Holiday and the musicians were given free rein to improvise. At first, studio executives didn't appreciate Holiday's improvisation of the melody line. They wanted her to sound more traditional, but when "What a Little Moonlight Can Do" became a modest hit, they relaxed and let her do her thing on future recordings.

Hammond promoted Holiday as a jazz musician. It was during these years that she established her distinctive singing and performing styles. She figured out what she could do and made some of her most famous recordings.

In these days, reviewers wrote about her distinctive **timbre**, her melodic inflections, and her unsentimental delivery. Her habit of rhythmic manipulation was already in place and would be discussed and written about for the rest of her career. She would enter a phrase two or three beats late, then catch up, then drop back again. Yet, as Miles Davis once commented, "A lot of singers try to sing like Billie, but just the act of playing behind the beat doesn't make it soulful."

She got mostly positive reviews, but once in a while she ran across somebody who didn't understand her style. Around the time she was making these recordings, she got a gig in Chicago with Fletcher Henderson's orchestra. The critics liked her. A reviewer in the *New York Age* wrote "you can't help but go for Billie Holiday songs." The club owner fired her, however, complaining that she sang too slowly.

A RISING STAR

The second phase of her career kicked off in 1939, when she began to sing "Strange Fruit." Although she never thought of herself as a political person or an activist, the song certainly carried that type of weight on its own. It also brought her to the public's attention as more than just a singer or an entertainer. She was mentioned in *Time* magazine, which may have helped sales of the controversial song. In terms of sales, "Strange Fruit" was the equivalent of a top twenty hit in the 1930s.

When she started to work more with Milt Gabler, Holiday took on show tunes and torch songs, pieces with more emotional content. She scored the biggest radio hit of her career during this phase with "Lover Man," the tune where Gabler had her accompanied by a full string orchestra. *Metronome* magazine's reviewer raved, "Billie has never been in better voice or better accompanied than on these sides … We're enthusiastic about the continued use of strings as a setting for her voice." A *New York Times* reviewer called her singing "pure enchantment" and another writer praised her show at New York's Town Hall by saying, "Gone was the moodiness … the reluctance to perform that [has] often made her a singer with no real love of her work.

At the recording studio in 1946

She was glad to be singing, perhaps no less than her audience was to be hearing her."

"Strange Fruit" made Billie Holiday a household name and brought her music to thousands more people. However, John Hammond did not think of this turning point as a positive. In addition to criticizing the song, he thought it made Holiday take herself too seriously. With "Strange Fruit," Hammond thought that Holiday lost her sparkle. He may very well have been right.

On the one hand, Holiday was now earning good money and making more decisions about her recording career. She voiced more opinions on what she sang, how she sang it, and what musicians she worked with. On the other hand, in doing so, she often demanded material that kept the focus on her. These decisions did not allow for much spontaneity or many solos by the musicians who backed her. She didn't improvise in the studio or onstage; she now performed as less of a singer and more of a "vocal actress." The songs she chose to sing had more emotional content and fuller musical settings, instead of the small jazz combos she used to work with. More and more, the songs she sang dealt with dramatic tension, heartbreak, or sadness.

While she was taking control of her career, she must have had some feelings of loss, too. Her relationship with John Hammond, who had been her champion for so long, was strained. She'd fought with Artie Shaw, who had been so good to her and tried to support and defend her when they had toured together. She was drinking more and taking more drugs. Was this the reason for her relationship problems? Or did the problems cause the substance abuse? Holiday had fallen into a vicious cycle.

Overall, 1943 was one of the best years in her career, though. She was singing at a Broadway nightclub called the Onyx. Musicians

LADY DAY

Billie Holiday was sometimes referred to as "Lady Day." She got the nickname from a close friend, saxophonist Lester Young, who she met in the early years of her career. The two were musical soul mates. Young's playing style—soft, with only a slight vibrato—matched Holiday's way of singing. Also like Holiday, he tried to tell a story with his horn. He preferred not to play songs exactly as written. One writer said, "To watch the two perform together was to see two artists who not only believed in each other, but through the sheer power of their music communicated on a level not often seen between two musicians."

Holiday had already picked up the nickname of "Lady" during her early days in the jazz clubs, when she refused to use the same raunchy methods as the other girls to pick up their tips. Young used the nickname affectionately, though. He also added "Day" as an abbreviation of "Holiday." In turn, Holiday nicknamed him "the President," or "Prez," because she said he was the world's greatest. Except for a three-year period where they didn't speak, their platonic and professional relationship lasted until Young's death in 1959, just four months before hers.

With musician Coleman Hawkins during a recording session, 1957

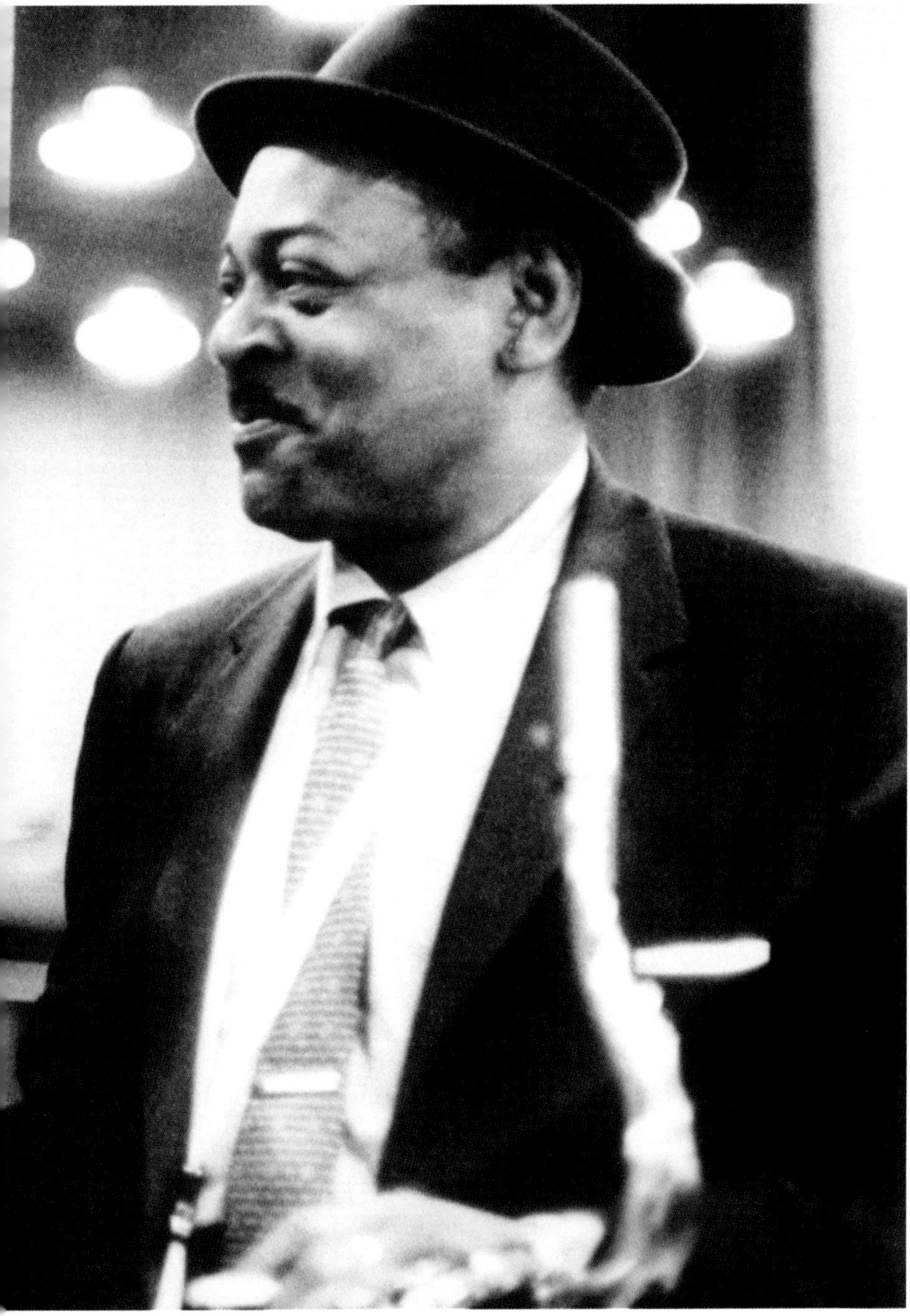

and fans alike called her "The Queen of 52nd Street." At the time, 52nd Street was often referred to simply as "The Street." It had a reputation as the place to be if you liked music. It held many restaurants and clubs. Most of the nightclubs were small—a tiny bandstand, a bar, a few tables and chairs—but people treated the whole area like an ongoing house party. They would travel from one club to another to see different musicians. Sometimes the musicians, once done with their sets, would join the stroll from club to club. Music journalist Stuart Nicholson commented, "The Street provided [Holiday] with an ideal forum; it allowed her talent to blossom." Frank Sinatra was said to have visited the Street to hear Holiday sing "as much as [he] could." It was in 1943 that, in a poll conducted by *Esquire* magazine, jazz critics voted Holiday the best jazz vocalist.

Unfortunately, toward the end of 1943, Holiday started dating a fellow musician, John Simmons, who was a known junkie. It wasn't long before people started to notice a difference in her personality and her performances. It may have been just after the start of their relationship that *Down Beat* magazine sniped, "Billie is not singing at her best in our opinion; nor does she sing often enough."

THE LATER YEARS

The third and final phase of Holiday's career was from 1949 to 1959. In the 1950s, popular jazz had begun to change. Swing and big band sounds were out. A new style called bebop was taking over. Sarah Vaughan and other bebop singers were becoming popular. Instead of trying to change and be more like them, Holiday re-recorded some of her early songs, giving them a new sound with

Holiday's onstage persona was elegant and vibrant at the peak of her career.

The Rollercoaster of Success

her more mature voice and changed outlook. They were better quality recordings, too, due to upgraded equipment. It turned out to be a blessing that she did this when she did, because by the late 1950s, she was in poor health, and her voice had started to change. Even when it was rough and weak, though, her vocal style didn't change much.

Holiday had long dreamed of touring Europe. She finally made it happen in 1954. She played in Sweden, Denmark, Norway, Germany, Switzerland, England, and France. She experienced great acclaim across the continent and tremendous audience adoration. The highlight of the tour was her final show, in London, playing to six thousand people at the Royal Albert Hall. She got rave reviews for this show, also.

When she returned to the states, she experienced another career highlight when she was asked to perform at the first Newport Jazz Festival. The organizers planned to showcase Holiday at the event. They put together a special band for the occasion: she was going to be backed by Teddy Wilson and several other musicians from her glory days at Columbia Records. That show was a triumph, and she was invited to participate in an all-star package tour. The tour included Count Basie and his orchestra, Sarah Vaughan, and Charlie Parker and his Modern Jazz Quartet. At one of these shows, Holiday either forgot her cue or couldn't remember which song she was supposed to sing at first. Once she burst into song, however, the crowd was wildly enthusiastic.

These large-scale jazz concerts, so popular in the 1950s, benefited her bank account and brought her music to larger audiences. But they couldn't make up for her inability to sing in New York City clubs. Concerts weren't something she could do every night, so she was not able to make a regular income or leverage her talent to further her career. Plus, the smaller venues better suited her style. Holiday had a small voice, and part of the attraction of seeing her in concert was her ability to create a connection with the audience. She couldn't do that on an open-air stage. Holiday vented about her banning to reporters in Britain. She pointed out that other performers had gotten in trouble for drugs and drinking but still had their cabaret cards. How their cases stacked up to hers is unknown.

Also in 1954, Holiday returned to Carnegie Hall. *Down Beat* magazine reviewed the show and commented that she seemed to be having an off night, but they weren't totally dismissive of her. They had recently given her a special award as "one of the great all-time vocalists in jazz." Holiday had never won one of their Best Singer polls, so she took pride in this award, knowing that it meant jazz critics and commentators thought highly of her and her talent.

It may have been at that show or another Carnegie Hall appearance around the same time that Holiday's drug use interfered with her performance. Pianist Oscar Peterson, who performed with her that night, commented that somebody must have "gotten to her" between sets. She'd sung beautifully for the first set, but during the second set, he remembers:

> I took one look at her and she was like the sphinx, like a graven image. I laid down the intro to "I Only Have Eyes for You." She missed the point where she was supposed to come in … I made a fast U-turn and went back, playing a more definitive intro, figuring she didn't hear the first one. She went right past that one, too. You could hear odd little whispers in the audience. God, it was horrible.

Holiday belts out a tune during a concert in Hamburg, Germany, in 1954.

Holiday did eventually start singing, but Peterson said, "She never went into tempo. We tried to find the time for her, but we couldn't lock her in, couldn't bring her back ... It didn't last long. Norman [Granz] came out and led her offstage."

Contrast that story to one that pianist Johnny Guarneri told about Holiday's time performing with him and the rest of Artie Shaw's band, about fifteen years earlier:

> The first night she handed me some tattered lead sheets and said, "Give me four bars." I played four bars. But she didn't come in. Figuring she hadn't heard me, or just missed her cue, I started over again. Suddenly I felt a tap on the back of my head, and I heard her say, "Don't worry 'bout me—I'll be there." She added that she liked to come in behind the beat, as I discovered, and that I didn't have to bother to make her look good. Looking back, I'd say that few performers had such a solid judgment about tempi as she did, particularly when it came to doing certain tunes in a very slow tempo ... Billie was the greatest tempo singer that ever lived."

Two years after that Carnegie Hall performance when Holiday had to be helped off the stage, she returned for another show where she had to be helped onto the stage. Journalist Gilbert Millstein remembered her husband, Louis McKay, and her manager, Joe Glaser, having to bring her in. She was apparently too drunk to walk. Millstein said her legs were swollen and she was almost incoherent. And yet, when she got out onto the stage, she nailed her performance. Millstein later wrote:

The lights went down, the musicians began to play and the narration began. Miss Holiday stepped from between the curtains, into the white spotlight awaiting her, wearing a white evening gown and white gardenias in her black hair. She was erect and beautiful; poised and smiling. And when the first section of the narration was ended, she sang—with strength undiminished—with all the art that was hers.

Nat Hentoff at *Down Beat* wrote of the same show:

Throughout the night, Billie was in superior form to what had sometimes been the case in the last years of her life. Not only was there assurance of phrasing and intonation; but there was also an outgoing warmth, a palpable eagerness to reach and touch the audience. And there was mocking wit. A smile was often lightly evident on her lips and her eyes as if, for once, she could accept the fact that there were people who did dig her. The beat flowed in her uniquely sinuous, supple way of moving the story along; the words became her own experiences; and coursing through it all was Lady's sound—a texture simultaneously steel-edged and yet soft inside; a voice that was almost unbearably wise in disillusion and yet still childlike, again at the centre. The audience was hers from before she sang, greeting her and saying good-bye with heavy, loving applause. And at one time, the musicians too applauded. It was a night when Billie was on top, undeniably the best and most honest jazz singer alive.

A recording was made that night and released as the album *The Essential Billie Holiday: Carnegie Hall Concert Recorded Live*. It backs up Millstein and Hentoff's assertions that Holiday could still put on a fantastic performance.

Later that year, however, Holiday was once again arrested for possession of narcotics. Her career and her health started a downward slide. While her performance at the 1958 Monterey Jazz Festival was met with applause and requests for encores, she tried to tour Europe again and was booed off the stage in Milan, Italy. She received mixed reviews in Paris. By the spring of 1959, she could no longer work regularly. She only took gigs when she felt healthy enough—which wasn't often.

Billie Holiday died in the summer of 1959, officially of congestion of the lungs complicated by heart failure, but unofficially of drug- and alcohol-related complications.

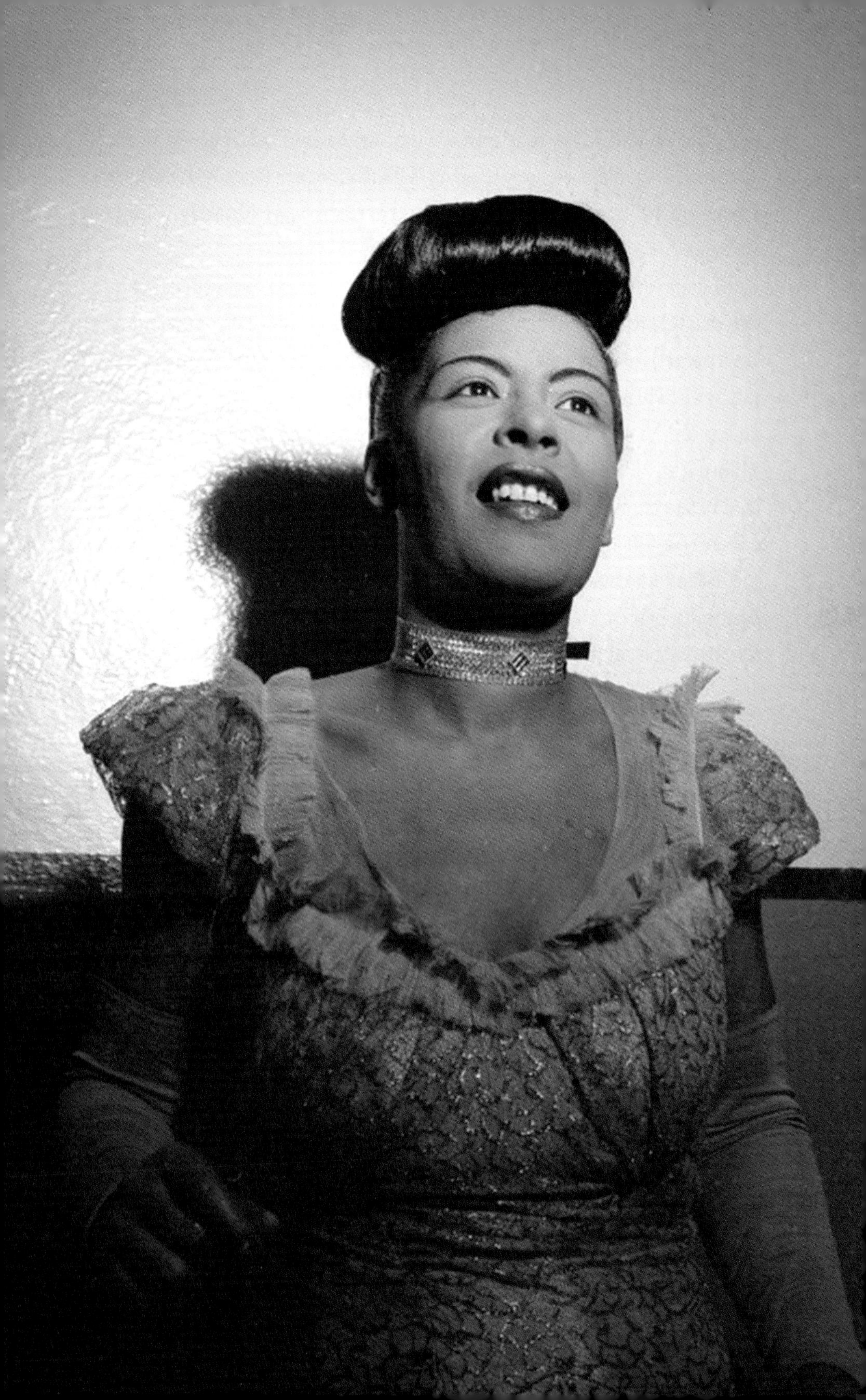

CHAPTER SIX

LADY DAY'S IMPACT

She only lived for forty-four years, but between her prodigious talent and her strong personality, Billie Holiday created a body of work and an image that have been influencing other artists for decades.

Frank Sinatra may have been one of the most famous singers to admit that Holiday had an effect on his own legendary career. "Billie was a good friend of mine," he once said. "She affected me in singing ... [She was] a great contributor to my career in the sense of articulating a song. She didn't know it and I didn't know it until it came to me later." Shortly before Holiday died, in a 1958 interview published in *Ebony* magazine, Sinatra said, "With few exceptions, every major pop singer in the United States during her generation has been touched in some way by her genius. It is Billie Holiday who was, and still remains, the greatest single

Opposite: Holiday, backstage at Carnegie Hall, sometime between 1946 and 1948

influence on me. Lady Day is unquestionably the most important influence on American popular singing in the last twenty years."

Many of her singing peers would probably agree. Peggy Lee, Rosemary Clooney, Dinah Washington, and Doris Day all said Holiday inspired or influenced them. In more recent years, artists like Sade, Macy Gray, Erykah Badu, Tori Amos, Madeleine Peyroux, and Amy Winehouse all owe their careers in some part to what Holiday achieved.

Carmen McRae, who was good friends with Holiday for many years, won the amateur singing contest at the Apollo Theater in 1939. She also wrote the song "Dream of Life," which Holiday recorded that same year. McRae had her own string of hits and a long career, but critics often remarked that her singing reminded them of Holiday's. McRae released an album of Holiday's classic songs in 1961, called *Carmen McRae Sings Lover Man & Other Billie Holiday Classics*.

Singer Nina Simone, after her death in 2003, was called "arguably the last of the great female jazz singers of her era." Simone always said that Holiday had a major musical influence on her life. She was brave enough to record her own version of "Strange Fruit" in 1968, and she later released an album called *Tribute to Billie Holiday*.

Other artists over the years have covered Holiday's signature songs, and some of them are rather unexpected. Reggae group UB40 recorded a version of "Strange Fruit." So did singer-songwriter Jeff Buckley. Stevie Wonder covered "God Bless the Child," and Elvis Costello sang "Gloomy Sunday" on his fifth album, *Trust*. Amy Winehouse released a rendition of "(There Is) No Greater Love" on her 2003 debut, *Frank*. And Herbie Hancock did "Don't Explain" with Damien Rice and Lisa Hannigan on his 2005 album *Possibilities*.

Because of her inability to get a cabaret card, toward the end of her career Holiday performed mostly at nightclubs outside New York City.

Lady Day's Impact

SONGS AND POEMS ABOUT BILLIE

It wasn't just other musicians that Holiday inspired. In 1959, New York poet Frank O'Hara was moved to write "The Day Lady Died," when he learned about Holiday's death while out running errands. A huge admirer of jazz and of Holiday in particular, O'Hara claimed to have written the poem on his lunch break. It ends with a memory of seeing her perform:

> thinking of
> leaning on the john door in the 5 SPOT
> while she whispered a song along the keyboard
> to Mal Waldron and everyone and I stopped breathing

Harlem Renaissance artist Langston Hughes also wrote a poem called "Song for Billie Holiday," which begins by asking:

> What can purge my heart
>   Of the song
>   And the sadness?
>
> What can purge my heart
>   But the song
>   Of the sadness?
>
> What can purge my heart
>   Of the sadness
>   Of the song?

The front page of the *Daily News* announces Billie's death; this is the newspaper that inspired Frank O'Hara's poem.

Lady Day's Impact   **101**

A MODERN MUSICAL TRIBUTE

Rock and roll fans may not even realize that Billie Holiday is the subject of what is probably the most popular song about her. Irish rock band U2's "Angel of Harlem" appeared on the 1988 album *Rattle and Hum*. The song calls her out by her nickname and creates an image of the beautiful but sad singer getting lost in the beautiful city:

> It was a cold and wet December day
> When we touched the ground at JFK
> Snow was melting on the ground
> On BLS I heard the sound
> Of an angel
>
> New York, like a Christmas tree
> Tonight this city belongs to me
> Angel
>
> … Lady Day got diamond eyes

She sees the truth behind the lies
Angel

… Blue light on the avenue
God knows they got to you
An empty glass, the lady sings
Eyes swollen like a bee sting
Blinded you lost your way
Through the side streets and the alleyway
Like a star exploding in the night
Falling to the city in broad daylight
An angel in Devil's shoes
Salvation in the blues
You never looked like an angel
Yeah yeah … angel of Harlem

Her old friend Frank Sinatra released a song called "Lady Day" in 1970. The song begins with the lyrics:

Her day was born in shades of blue
Her song was sad, the words were true
Her morning came too fast, too soon
And died before the afternoon

Poor lady day could use some love, some sunshine
Lady day has too much rain
Poor lady day could use some spring, some breezes
Lady day has too much pain

As an aside, Frank Sinatra's valet claims that Sinatra cried when Billie Holiday died. He reportedly visited her in the hospital just hours before she passed away.

AWARDS AND PERFORMANCE TRIBUTES

Only two years after her death, *Down Beat* magazine voted Holiday into their Hall of Fame. Her 1941 recording of "God Bless the Child" entered the Grammy Hall of Fame in 1976. Holiday was the first woman to receive that honor. She received twenty-two posthumous Grammy nominations, with six wins. In 1987, she was awarded the National Academy of Recording Arts and Science's Lifetime Achievement Award. "Strange Fruit" was listed in the Library of Congress's National Recording Registry in 2002. In 2000, she was inducted into the Rock and Roll Hall of Fame, named as an early influence, in honor of the countless performers she made an impact on.

Diana Ross handled her induction into the Hall of Fame. Ross famously played Holiday in the movie version of *Lady Sings the Blues*. Ross received a Golden Globe award and an Oscar nomination. The film's soundtrack went to number one on the Billboard Hot 200 Album Charts for two weeks.

Holiday was portrayed in a nightclub scene in the Denzel Washington film *Malcolm X*, played by actress Miki Howard. Howard later released an album called *Miki Sings Billie: A Tribute to Billie Holiday*.

In the 1980s, a play called *Lady Day at Emerson's Bar & Grill* premiered at the Alliance Theatre in Atlanta, Georgia. The premise of the play is that Holiday is performing in a run-down bar, shortly before her death in July 1959. She sings and tells stories about her life. After its run in Atlanta, the show opened off-Broadway, where it won an Outer Critics Circle Award. Both Lonette McKee and S. Epatha Merkerson played Holiday during its off-Broadway run. The show returned to Broadway in 2014, and actress Audra McDonald won a record-breaking sixth Tony Award for her portrayal of Holiday. During her acceptance speech, McDonald said, "I want to thank all the shoulders of the strong and brave and courageous women that I am standing on ... and most of all, Billie Holiday. You deserve so much more than you were given when you were on this planet. This is for you."

CENTENNIAL TRIBUTES

In 2015, the jazz community celebrated Billie Holiday's hundredth birthday in a number of ways. Performers across the globe paid tribute to her talent in song and at special events. She even got her own hashtag: #Billieat100. Many of the events took place in spring, close to her birthdate of April 7.

The renowned Jazz at Lincoln Center program announced their plans to honor her by stating, "Billie Holiday is a profound influence on everyone who wants to sing jazz music, and we wanted to make sure we celebrated her in a way that was true to her spirit."

Jazz vocalist Cécile McLorin Salvant performed four sets of Holiday's songs during two concerts in April at Lincoln Center, as part of their centennial celebration of Holiday's birthday. Other events included a show called "Celebrating Lady Day" with performances by vocalists Andy Bey, Molly Johnson, and Sarah Elizabeth Charles. An eight-piece band performed her songs with various vocalists at Dizzy's Club Coca-Cola. Salvant, only twenty-five years old, was chosen because "her youth made her a fitting person to help ground Ms. Holiday's influence in the present and suggest its continued relevance."

Columbia University professor Farah Jasmine Griffin, who published a cultural study of Holiday called *If You Can't Be Free, Be a Mystery* in 2001, said, "That so many still find it important to celebrate Ms. Holiday speaks to the breadth and virtuosity of her work." Griffin participated in a panel with two other authors in spring 2015 called "When the Moon Turns Green: The Myth and Music of Billie Holiday." Griffin once collaborated on a show at the Apollo Theater based on Holiday's music and the writings of Harlem Renaissance author Zora Neale Hurston with singer Queen Esther. Esther performed a series of shows in honor of Billie Holiday's birthday in Harlem in April 2015, called "Queen Esther Sings Billie Holiday: The Rare Sides."

Audra McDonald won a Tony award for her portrayal of Billie Holiday in *Lady Day at Emerson's Bar & Grill* in 2014.

Lady Day's Impact **107**

One of the murals created in Billie Holiday's honor in her hometown of Baltimore, Maryland

In London, in March 2015, soul singer Rebecca Ferguson performed her version of the iconic album *Lady Sings the Blues* in tribute. Baltimore, Holiday's hometown, re-created Holiday's 1956 Carnegie Hall concert. It starred jazz vocalist Denyse Pearson, backed by Charm City's own Arch Social Club Big Band. The city of Baltimore also sponsored a Billie Holiday Arts Project that created a citywide tribute to her music and her life. Screens featuring themes and images from Holiday's life and music were painted on several houses on her old street. Baltimore artist Joe Rizza created a mosaic, and several local artists painted murals. Local children honored Holiday's trademark hair decoration by painting gardenias on various walls around the city.

Other cities got in on the act as well. In Austin, Texas, the Women in Jazz concert series created a show called "Café Society Celebrates Billie Holiday's 100th Birthday." Singer Pamela Hart portrayed Holiday as she was during the years she performed at the Café Society nightclub in Greenwich Village. St. Philip's College in San Antonio and the Twin City Stage in Winston-Salem both revived *Lady Day at Emerson's Bar & Grill*. The Charleston Jazz Orchestra performed an entire concert dedicated to Holiday and her music. In Denver, jazz vocalist Venus Cruz honored Holiday's role in American history and jazz's place in Denver's story by putting on a tribute concert.

Back in New York City, the club Minton's in Harlem, where Holiday once performed, staged a show called "Billie Holiday Turns 100 at Minton's." The Apollo Theater celebrated the singer's birthday by inducting her into their Walk of Fame. They installed the plaque with her name right underneath the Apollo's marquee. As part of that ceremony, Grammy-winning jazz singer Cassandra Wilson gave a concert. Wilson also released an album in tribute

Charm City jazz musician Wade Johnson performs at the rededication ceremony for the Billie Holiday statue in Baltimore.

Lady Day's Impact

to Holiday. On *Coming Forth By Day*, she puts her own spin on eleven of Holiday's songs, including "Billie's Blues," "What a Little Moonlight Can Do," and "Strange Fruit."

Another album released in 2015 in honor of Billie Holiday comes from a male singer. José James put out *Yesterday I Had The Blues: The Music of Billie Holiday* as a tribute to the woman he refers to as his musical mother. The album includes nine songs written by or popularized by Holiday, such as "Lover Man" and "God Bless the Child." Like Wilson, he also offers his interpretations of "What a Little Moonlight Can Do" and "Strange Fruit."

The Philadelphia Music Alliance put her name on their Walk of Fame on the Avenue of the Arts. Philadelphia is where Holiday was actually born. Meanwhile, Columbia Records/Legacy Recordings released *The Centennial Collection*, an anthology of twenty of Holiday's finest recordings.

Finally, as part of their birthday tribute, *Baltimore* magazine asked several Baltimore musicians to name their favorite song from Holiday's canon. Each of the respondents had made a personal connection with Holiday's music. Jack Everly, principal pops conductor of the Baltimore Symphony Orchestra, chose "Remember." He said that its haunting lyrics and melody made her performance especially poignant. Lea Gilmore, a jazz and blues vocalist, chose "Strange Fruit." Gilmore admired Holiday's bravery at performing the song during a period of deep racism. She also praised Holiday for her understated delivery of the painful topic.

OTHER TRIBUTES

The United States Postal Service issued a stamp featuring Holiday's image in 1994. Announcing the stamp, they called her "one of

The US Postal Service issued a Billie Holiday stamp in 1994.

the most influential jazz singers of all time." In the city where Holiday grew up, Baltimore, Maryland, there is a statue of her at the corner of Pennsylvania and Lafayette Avenues. It is near the site of the Royal Theatre, where Holiday often performed. The statue depicts her wearing a strapless gown, with her trademark gardenias in her hair, her mouth open in song. Around the granite base are panels depicting symbols of racism, including a crow eating a gardenia. The sculptor said it "represents the Jim Crow racism that ate the spirit of black people, including Billie Holiday."

All of this was in tribute to a woman who always downplayed her talent. In a home recording, Holiday said of herself:

Lady Day's Impact   **113**

At the beginning of her career, it was Holiday's turn to be out and about in the Harlem nightlife wearing a fur coat.

> I'm telling you, me and my old voice, it just go up a little bit and come down a little bit. It's not legit; I do not got a legitimate voice. This voice of mine is a mess, a cat got to know what he's doing when he plays with me.

Holiday always claimed that she stumbled into singing, and in a way that's true. Like many artists of the era, she had no technical training and could not read music. She was just a natural singer and performer. And yet, as David Graham wrote in the *Atlantic*, "What accounts for her longevity? For one thing, she's arguably the greatest jazz singer ever. She's certainly the most familiar. Even people who can't tell Ella Fitzgerald from Peggy Lee know that voice, so recognizable and so difficult to describe."

It may have been because her voice was so full of expression. It may have been because she considered her voice an instrument, like a horn, and she mimicked the sounds of the other horns. It may be because she wanted to communicate with the audience more than she wanted to entertain them. Pulitzer Prize–nominated poet Maya Angelou once wrote, "Billie Holiday was a keen observer. She saw through lyrics and she saw through people. And she chose what and who she wanted. She sang every song not only as if she had written it herself, but as if she had written it that very morning."

Somehow, this girl from the tough streets of Baltimore, born on the wrong side of the blanket and the wrong side of the tracks, became a legend. She was one of a kind.

CHRONOLOGY

1915 Born on April 7 in Philadelphia to unwed mother Sadie Harris/Fagan.

1922 Sent to reform school for wayward girls.

1929 Moves to New York City to live with her mother; arrested for solicitation and sent to jail on Welfare Island.

1930 Starts singing in clubs and speakeasies to earn money; changes name to Billie Holiday.

1933 Catches the attention of John Hammond and begins her recording career.

1934 Performs at Harlem's famed Apollo Theater for the first time.

1935 Signs on with manager Joe Glaser.

1937 Meets Lester Young, who nicknames her Lady Day; joins the Count Basie Orchestra on tour.

1939 Quits Count Basie's band and joins Artie Shaw's.

1939 Records and releases "Strange Fruit."

1941 Marries Jimmy Monroe.

1945 Sadie Fagan dies.

1946 Appears in the movie *New Orleans*.

1947 Checks herself into rehab for heroin addiction; arrested later the same year for heroin possession.

1949 Arrested twice, once for assault and once for possession.

1951 Meets Louis McKay.

1954 Tours Europe.

1956 Arrested again for narcotics possession; publishes an autobiography called *Lady Sings the Blues*.

1959 Passes away from the effects of drug and alcohol abuse.

HOLIDAY'S MOST IMPORTANT WORKS

ALBUMS

The Quintessential Billie Holiday, Volumes 3 and 4 (1936–1937)
Billie Holiday (1946)
Billie Holiday–Teddy Wilson: A Hot Jazz Classic Set, Vol. 1 (1947)
Teddy Wilson and His Orchestra Featuring Billie Holiday (1949)
Lover Man (1951)
Billie Holiday Sings (1952)
Lady Day (1954)
The Lady Sings (1956)
Lady Sings the Blues (1956)
Ella Fitzgerald and Billie Holiday at Newport (1957)
Carnegie Hall Concert (1961)
Lady in Satin (1958)
The Complete Billie Holiday on Verve 1945–1959 (1992)

GLOSSARY

blue blood A member of a noble or socially prominent family.

brothel A building in which prostitutes are available.

cold turkey The act of stopping a bad habit (such as taking drugs) in a sudden and complete way.

communism A way of organizing a society in which the government owns the things that are used to make and transport products (such as land, oil, factories, ships, etc.) and there is no privately owned property.

conventional Used and accepted by most people; usual or traditional.

cosmopolitan Sophisticated; containing a diverse group of people from a variety of places and backgrounds.

encore An extra piece of music performed in response to a request from the audience.

fascism A way of organizing a society in which a government ruled by a dictator controls the lives of the people and in which people are not allowed to disagree with the government.

heinous Very bad or evil; deserving of hate or contempt.

illegitimate Born to a father and mother who are not married.

integrated Allowing all types of people to participate or be included; not segregated.

Jim Crow laws Any of the laws that enforced racial segregation in the South between the end of Reconstruction in 1877 and the beginning of the civil rights movement in the 1950s.

longshoreman A person whose job is to load and unload ships at a port.

lynching To put to death (as by hanging) by mob action without legal authority.

oppression Unjust or cruel exercise of authority or power.

pantheon A group of people who are famous or important.

pneumonia A serious disease that affects the lungs and makes it difficult to breathe.

prenatal Relating to pregnant women and their unborn babies.

slovenly Messy or untidy.

timbre The quality of the sound made by a particular voice or musical instrument.

ultimatum A promise that force or punishment will be used if someone does not do what is wanted.

vibrato A way of making small, rapid changes in a musical note that you are singing or playing so that it seems to shake slightly.

wedlock The state of being married.

FURTHER INFORMATION

BOOKS

Blackburn, Julia. *With Billie*. New York, NY Pantheon Books, 2005.

Chilton, John. *Billie's Blues: The Billie Holiday Story 1933–1959*. New York, NY: Da Capo Press, 1975.

Clarke, Donald. Billie Holiday: Wishing on the Moon. New York, NY: Da Capo Press, 2000.

Gourse, Leslie. *The Billie Holiday Companion: Seven Decades of Commentary*. New York, NY: Schirmer, 1997.

Holiday, Billie, with William Dufty. *Lady Sings the Blues*. New York, NY: Penguin Books, 1956.

O'Meally, Robert. *Lady Day: The Many Faces of Billie Holiday*. New York, NY: Da Capo Press, 1991.

WEBSITES

American Masters: Billie Holiday
www.pbs.org/wnet/americanmasters/episodes/billie-holiday/about-the-singer/68
PBS's Billie Holiday page offers a concise biographical sketch.

Billie Holiday – Biography
www.biography.com/people/billie-holiday-9341902
Biography.com features an informative summary of the singer's life.

The Official Website of Billie Holiday
www.billieholiday.com
The official Billie Holiday website features photos, videos, and biographical information. The site launched the #BillieAt100 Twitter campaign in honor of Lady Day's centennial in 2015.

The Unofficial Billie Holiday Website
www.ladyday.net
This website includes lists of suggested reading and listening, as well as links to information about Holiday and her various musical collaborators.

BIBLIOGRAPHY

Biography.com Editors. "Billie Holiday." Accessed September 28, 2015. http://www.biography.com/people/billie-holiday-9341902#related-video-gallery.

Blackburn, Julia. *With Billie*. New York, NY: Pantheon Books, 2005.

Blair, Elizabeth. "Looking For Lady Day's Resting Place? Detour Ahead." NPR, July 17, 2012. Accessed September 28, 2015. http://www.npr.org/2012/07/17/156686608/looking-for-lady-days-resting-place-detour-ahead.

Cole, Forrest. *Billie Holiday, Singer.* Black Americans of Achievement. New York, NY: Chelsea House, 2011.

Gioia, Ted. *The History of Jazz*. New York, NY: Oxford University Press, 1997.

Gourse, Leslie. *The Billie Holiday Companion: Seven Decades of Commentary*. New York, NY: Schirmer, 1997.

Greene, Meg. *Billie Holiday: A Biography*. Greenwood Biographies. Westport, CT: Greenwood Press, 2007.

Ingham, Chris. *Billie Holiday.* Divas. New York, NY: Welcome Rain Publishers, 2000.

Jones, Hettie. *Big Star Fallin' Mama: Five Women in Black Music*. New York, NY: Viking Press, 1995.

McDonough, John. "Billie Holiday: A Singer Beyond Our Understanding." NPR, April 7, 2015. Accessed September 28, 2015. http://www.npr.org/2015/04/07/397877385/billie-holiday-a-singer-beyond-our-understanding.

New York Times. "Billie Holiday Dies Here at 44; Jazz Singer Had Wide Influence." *New York Times*, July 18, 1959. Accessed September 28, 2015. http://www.nytimes.com/learning/general/onthisday/bday/0407.html.

Nicholson, Stuart. *Billie Holiday*. Boston: Northeastern University Press, 1995.

"Official Website of Billie Holiday, The." Accessed September 28, 2015. http://www.billieholiday.com.

PBS. "Billie Holiday: The Long Night of Lady Day." PBS, June 8, 2006. Accessed September 28, 2015. http://www.pbs.org/wnet/americanmasters/billie-holiday-about-the-singer/68/.

Szwed, John. *Billie Holiday: The Musician and the Myth*. New York, NY: Viking, 2015.

Vitale, Tom. "Billie Holiday: Emotional Power Through Song." NPR, November 22, 2010. Accessed September 28, 2015. http://www.npr.org/2010/11/19/131451449/billie-holiday-emotional-power-through-song.

Ward, Geoffrey C., and Ken Burns. *Jazz: A History of America's Music*. New York, NY: Alfred A. Knopf, 2000.

INDEX

Page numbers in **boldface** are illustrations. Entries in **boldface** are glossary terms.

Apollo Theater, 31–32, 72, 98, 106, 109
Armstrong, Louis, 7, 16, 19–20, **21**, 38, 80

Basie, Count, 33, 51, **52–53**, 54, 58, 90
blue blood, 33
brothel, 16, 25–26

Carnegie Hall, 20, 48, 91, 93–95, **96**, 109
cold turkey, 46–47
communism, 70
conventional, 8
cosmopolitan, 12

Ellington, Duke, 7, 16, 35–36, **37**
encore, 32, 73, 95

fascism, 70

Goodman, Benny, 34–35, 80
"God Bless the Child," 64–67, **65**, 98, 104, 112

Hammond, John, 32–35, **34**, 39, 63, 67, 73, 80–81, 84
Harris, Sadie, 9, 11–14, 16, 26–27, 30, **40**, 41–42, 45–46, 65–66, 73
heinous, 16
Henderson, Bobby, 30–31, 39, 42
Herzog, Arthur, Jr., 64–67
Holiday, Billie
　career, 20, 25, 27–28, 30–39, 50–51, **52–53**, 54–55, 58, **62**, **74–75**, **78**, 80–82, 83, 84, **86–87**, 88, **89**, 90–91, **92**, 93–95, **96**, 99
　critical reception, 33, 36, 41, 73, 76–77, 81–82, 84, 88, 90–91, 94–95
　early life, 8–9, **10**, 12–14, 16, 19
　influences, 7, **15**, 16, 19–23, **21**, **22**

126　　Billie Holiday

legacy, 41, 77, 79, 97–98, 100, 102–106, **108**, 109, **110**–**111**, 112–113, **113**, 115
legal troubles, 14, 16, 19, **24**, 26–27, 43, 45–50, 73, 95
marriages, 46, **47**, **56**–**57**, 58–59
race and, 50–51, 54–55, 58
singing style, 19–20, **71**, 79, 81, 90, 93–94, 114
songs, 20, 23, 35–37, 63–70, **65**, 72–73, 76–77, 80–82, 84, 112
Holiday, Clarence, 9, 11–12, 14, 16, 28, 30, 42
Hughes, Langston, 26, 100

illegitimate, 9, 11, 13
integrated, 30

Jim Crow laws, 8, 55, **55**, 113

Lady Day at Emerson's Bar & Grill, 105, **107**, 109
longshoreman, 14
"Lover Man," 67–69, **68**, 82, 98, 112
lynching, 69–70, 73, 76

McKay, Louis, **56**–**57**, 59, 93
Meeropol, Abel, 70, 72
Monroe, Jimmy, 46, **47**, 58–59

O'Hara, Frank, 100, **101**
oppression, 8

pantheon, 25
pneumonia, 42
prenatal, 12

Shaw, Artie, 51, 54, 58, 84, 93
Simone, Nina, 77, 98
Sinatra, Frank, 88, 97–98, 104
slovenly, 11
Smith, Bessie, 7, **15**, 16, 19, 20–23, **22**, 79
"Strange Fruit," 69–70, 72–73, 76–77, 82, 84, 98, 104, 112

timbre, 81

ultimatum, 30

vibrato, 19–20, 85

wedlock, 9
Wilson, Teddy, 35, 38–39, **38**, 63, 81, 90

ABOUT THE AUTHOR

Rebecca Carey Rohan lives in upstate New York with her two children and three rescued pets. She is the author of *Working with Electricity: Electrical Engineers*, *Great American Thinkers: Thurgood Marshall*, and two other titles in the Artists of the Harlem Renaissance series, *Duke Ellington* and *Langston Hughes*.